Praise for *Debugging Teams*

"With honest clarity, Fitz and Ben have put together a manual for developing great products. But this is not a technical manual. Its key insight is that great products start (and end) with the people and organizations that build them. A great read for makers of any stripe."

—Nicole Wong, Former White House Deputy Chief Technology Officer for Internet and Innovation Policy

"This delicious book speaks to your inner geek! Even if you do not consider yourself a geek, the advice is worth the time to read anyway."

—Vint Cerf, Chief Internet Evangelist at Google

"Software development is a team sport. If you want to become a top performer in the sport, there are hundreds of good books that tell you how to work on your individual skills as a software developer, and a few on how to be a good manager. This book breaks new ground by setting out all the key lessons for you as a software developer to learn how to work with your teammates, and how to be a good teammate. The field has needed a book like this for a long time, and finally it has arrived."

—Peter Norvig, Director of Research at Google

"I've been working with engineers for over 30 years, and in that time I've learned that engineering is as much about people as it is science and technology, but most engineers put little or no effort into understanding how to work with others. If you want to be more effective and efficient at creating and innovating, then this book is for you."

—Dean Kamen, Founder of DEKA Research

"This is a wonderful book. It deals with the hardest problem in computer programming, which is dealing with other computer programmers :-). I'll be buying copies for all Samba team members."

—Jeremy Allison, Cocreator of Samba

"You might have heard the aphorism '10X programmer,' describing the fact that top programmers are an order of magnitude more productive than average programmers. Making a big impact requires experience and powerful technical chops, but also empathy for your coworkers and users. No amount of smarts or knowledge can make up for a lack of the latter, but this book will help you hone your soft skills and leave an even bigger dent in the world."

—Bob Lee, Former Chief Technology Officer at Square

"In Debugging Teams, Fitz and Ben have drawn on their deep and broad experiences as highly regarded programmers to lay out, in a very readable and entertaining way, the keys to success for any sort of team-based creative endeavor—in other words, any company! It's full of useful insights in areas related to leadership, collaboration, problem solving and communication. Anyone who cares about being more productive and more successful—in both their professional and their personal lives—will benefit from reading this book. It's a great example of the power of combining analytics and human insights.

—Christie Hefner, Former CEO of Playboy, Inc.

"Fitz and Ben take a simple creed—Humility, Respect, and Trust—and cultivate that foundation with copious examples and stories. The experience and wisdom they share will help software engineers who work in teams—most of us—be more effective and productive."

—Greg J. Badros, CEO of Prepared Mind Innovations

"Software is made of people. A well-run team, using the principles outlined in Debugging Teams, can out-think, out-code, and out-ship any individual hacker. Coder, educate thyself!"

—Johnathan Nightingale, Chief Product Officer at Hubba

"Debugging Teams *is a gem of a book, in which Ben and Fitz share their very sensible philosophy of how programmers can best contribute to a good team. We are lucky that this important field is finally opened up for discussion with such warmth and humor. I wish that 21-year-old me had both a copy of the book and the good sense to take it to heart.*"

—Bryan O'Sullivan, Facebook

"*This book is a blueprint for building a healthy software development culture. It should be required reading for engineering managers, technical leaders, and even nontechnical executives who need to understand how team dynamics affect retention of top engineering talent and the quality of software they produce.*"

—Bruce Johnson, Founder and Chief Operating Officer at FullStory

"*The skill of writing software will help you stay employed, but if you combine that with the ability to work well with others, you can change the world. This book isn't just about how you can be a better programmer. It's about how to be awesome.*"

—Clay Johnson, Author of
The Information Diet

"Debugging Teams *is an insightful exploration of building successful teams and products, taken from years of tackling difficult developer pains and issues that we all experience in our careers. The jovial approach to overcoming both engineering and human issues on a technical team delivers an engaging foundation text that should be a staple of every engineer's library.*"

—Jonathan LeBlanc, Head of Global Developer Advocacy at PayPal

"*Programming is no longer about code and machines, if it ever was. Increasingly, it's about fitting together existing pieces in new ways—and each piece comes with people attached. The authors have understood this for years, and their message is as simple as their advice is varied: focus on the people as much as you focus on the code, and you will not only be a happier programmer, you will be the cause of happier programmers. It couldn't come at a better time!*"

—Karl Fogel, Cofounder of Open Tech Strategies LLC

From Ben

*For my parents, bringers of hope and joy, who taught me
how to read both words and people.*

From Fitz

*For my grandfather, Alvin "Nick" Fitzpatrick, who taught me
how to tell stories, and how to listen.*

Contents

Mission Statement

The goal of this book is to help people spend more time creating and less time fighting—by improving their ability to collaborate with other people.

Acknowledgments

While there are two names on the cover, this book is the result of conversations we've had with hundreds if not thousands of people over the course of our lives and careers. We'd like to take a few moments to thank just a few of the people who are responsible for many of the useful parts of this book (mistakes, as usual, are all ours).

Thanks to the folks at O'Reilly Media: Mike Loukides for encouraging us to write for a broader audience, and our fearless editors Brian Anderson and Mary Treseler—this book wouldn't exist without Mary's encouragement, patience, and occasional prodding.

Thanks to Sunni Brown and Amber Lewis at *http://sunnibrown.com* for bringing our book to life with such delightful illustrations—working with you guys was a true joy.

Thanks to our technical reviewers who contributed numerous suggestions, ideas, and fixes that really brought the book together: Dustin Boswell, Trevor Foucher, Michael Hunger, Jonathan LeBlanc, Piaw Na, and Jack Welch. Thanks to our friends and colleagues who reviewed the book in progress and caught some of our more egregious mistakes: Dave Baum, Matt Cutts, Will Robinson, and Bill Duane. Thanks to our friends who listened, offered advice, and are just plain awesome: Karl Fogel, Jim Blandy, Matt Braithwaite, Danny Berlin, and Chris DiBona. Thanks also to Linda Stone, DeWitt Clinton, Bruce Johnson, Roland McGrath, and Amit Patel for ideas and suggestions.

Thanks to Google, and especially the Google Chicago engineering team, for their support, ideas, and suggestions, and for just plain being a fantastic group of people to work with every day.

Thanks especially to some of our senior mentors and teachers, a tiny bit of whose collective wisdom we've attempted to squeeze onto these pages: Bill Coughran, Steve Vinter, Alan Eustace, Stu Feldman, and Eric Schmidt.

Special thanks to Brian Robinson and Yvonne Ellison-Sandler for their mentoring, guidance, and tutelage.

Thanks to the Apache Software Foundation, not only for having us, but also for your focus on community and collaboration.

Thanks to all our close friends, who make us rich, rich men. Don't look at us that way—you know who you are.

Huge swaths of this book were conceived, outlined, and written at the fabulous, friendly, and cozy Filter Cafe in our fair city of Chicago.

From Fitz

Huge thanks to my wife Marie for her encouragement, understanding, and patience—your insight and compassion are always an inspiration to me. Thanks to my mom for her support and enthusiasm, and thanks especially to my mother-in-law Rita Gumler, for her "people are like plants" analogy.

To Ben: after knowing each other for 16 years, working together at three jobs, and writing three books together, I have to say that I miss working with you every day. Thanks for taking this wild, weird, and wonderful ride with me—you've been a great friend and teacher.

Lastly, thanks to everyone that I've worked with in my (gulp) 21 years in software engineering. It's been an incredible journey, and not a day has gone by where I didn't learn something from one of you.

From Ben

There aren't proper words to express my gratitude for the amount of space my wife Frances has given me—not just in writing this book, but in a dozen other creative projects I've taken on over the past few years. Without her quiet and rocklike support, none of them could possibly have happened.

To Fitz: now that we finish each other's sentences I think it's fair to say we're like a very old married couple. I never knew it could be so much fun to give talks with somebody, let alone write software and books together. What an amazing set of opportunities we've been given! Thanks for teaching me so much.

Finally, thanks to all the crazy people and corporations of Silicon Valley: none of these crazy experiences could have happened if you hadn't inducted me into your bizarro-world.

About the Authors

Brian Fitzpatrick is Founder and CTO of Tock. Brian started Google's Chicago engineering office with Ben in 2005 and led several of Google's global engineering efforts, including the Data Liberation Front, and Transparency Engineering. He also served as internal advisor for Google's open data efforts, having previously led the Google Code and Google Affiliate Network teams. Prior to joining Google, Brian worked as an engineer at Apple, CollabNet, and a local Chicago development shop.

Brian has written numerous articles and given dozens of presentations, including cowriting *Team Geek: A Software Developer's Guide to Working Well with Others*, *Version Control with Subversion* (now in its second edition), and chapters for *Unix in a Nutshell* and *Linux in a Nutshell*.

Brian has an A.B. in Classics from Loyola University Chicago with a major in Latin, a minor in Greek, and a concentration in Fine Arts and Ceramics. He resides in Chicago.

Ben Collins-Sussman was one of the founding developers of the Subversion version control system. He cofounded Google's engineering office in Chicago, launched Google Code, led two display advertising teams, and now manages teams that power Google's search infrastructure. He's currently the engineering Site Lead for Google Chicago, but also collects hobbies—including authoring interactive fiction, playing bluegrass banjo and jazz piano, composing musicals, operating ham radios, and exploring photography. Ben is a proud native of Chicago and holds a Bachelor of Science from the University of Chicago with a major in Mathematics and minor in Linguistics. He still lives in Chicago with his wife, kids, and cats.

Foreword to the Second Edition

The first edition of this book, *Team Geek*, proved to be a great success. In the four years since it was published there seems to be more widespread recognition of the importance of teamwork in business. In some places, collaboration is now being taught as part of college curriculums and leadership training classes (often using our book!).

But we also came to realize that the first edition of the book was perhaps a bit too focused on software engineering, so we've expanded this second edition to be more accessible to a nontechnical audience—hence the title change to *Debugging Teams*. While we still draw on engineering examples, there's less focus on nitty-gritty details of software development tools. We've expanded and generalized a number of our explanations throughout the book based on continuous feedback from readers. We've also added sections on more recent topics, such as open seating plans, imposter syndrome, and newer communication and leadership techniques.

We hope this expansion will have a broader appeal and impact across multiple industries.

—Ben and Fitz,
September 2015

Introduction

Engineering is easy. People are hard.

—Bill Coughran,
former senior vice president of engineering at Google

Life is full of unexpected twists, and the two of us never imagined we'd someday write a book about teamwork and collaboration.

Like so many modern "makers," we discovered that our hobby and passion—playing with computers—was a great way to make a living after graduating college. And like most hackers of our generation, we spent the mid-1990s building PCs out of spare parts, installing prerelease versions of Linux from piles of diskettes, and learning to administer Unix machines. At the dawn of the dot-com bubble we became programmers, and after the bubble burst we started working for surviving Silicon Valley companies such as Apple. Later, we were hired by a startup to work full time on designing and writing an open source version control system called Subversion.

But something unexpected happened between 2000 and 2005. While we were creating Subversion, our job responsibilities slowly changed. We weren't just writing code all day in a vacuum; we were leading an open source project. This meant hanging in a chat room all day with a dozen other volunteer programmers and paying attention to what they were doing. It meant coordinating new features almost entirely through an email list. Along the way, we discovered that the key to a project's success wasn't just writing great code: the *way* in which people collaborated toward the end goal mattered just as much.

In 2005 we started Google's Chicago engineering office and continued our careers as programmers. At this point we were already deeply involved with the open source world—not just Subversion, but the Apache Software Foundation

(ASF) too. We ported Subversion to Google's BigTable infrastructure and launched an open source project hosting service (similar to SourceForge) under the banner of Google Code. We began attending—then speaking at—developer-centric conferences such as OSCON, ApacheCon, PyCon, and eventually Google I/O. We discovered that by working in both corporations and open source projects we had accidentally picked up a trove of wisdom and anecdotes about how real software engineering teams work. What began as a series of humorous talks about dysfunctional development processes ("Subversion Worst Practices") eventually turned into talks about protecting teams from jerks ("How Open Source Projects Survive Poisonous People"). Larger and larger crowds gathered at our presentations in what can only be described as "group therapy" for software developers.

After giving talk after talk about the social challenges of creative collaboration, our editor at O'Reilly Media encouraged us to convert the talks into a book. The rest is history.

Who Is This Book For?

This book was originally written for software developers—for those who are trying to advance their careers and ship great software. But in updating the book for a second edition, it has become clear to us that the topics in this book apply to a much broader group. If you work on *any* sort of creative endeavor with other people, the lessons in this book apply to you. You might be part of a neighborhood club, a church group, a fraternity, a committee, or a group of architects. We're assuming two important things about you as our reader:

- You work on a team with other creative people, probably in a corporate or other structured environment.

- You enjoy building things and believe it should be a rewarding and fun activity. If you're cranking out products for no other reason than to pay your bills, you probably aren't interested in self-actualization or career fulfillment.

Our own experiences come from software engineering, so predictably most of the examples in this book live in that realm. But nearly all the processes and strategies we describe are directly applicable (or have a direct analogue) to any team of creative people.

In the process of discussing how engineers best "play well with others," we end up touching on a number of subjects that (superficially) may seem to be out of a programmer's job description. At different points we discuss how to lead a team effectively, navigate an organization, and build a healthy relationship with the users of your software. On the surface these chapters may seem specifically directed toward "people managers" or "product managers"—but we assure you that at some point in your career you'll find yourself accidentally wearing those hats. Suspend your disbelief and keep reading! Everything in this book is ultimately relevant to anyone building things.

WARNING: THIS IS NOT A TECHNICAL MANUAL

Before we start, we need to set your expectations. Motivated programmers love to read books that lay out domain-specific problems in a perfect mathematical presentation; each problem is typically paired with a prescribed procedural solution. This is not such a book.

Our book specifically investigates the *human* side of creative product development, and humans are complex things. As we like to say in our talks, "People are basically a giant pile of intermittent bugs." Both the problems and solutions we discuss are messy and difficult to place into perfect logical boxes. This book reads as a series of essays, because that's what it essentially is. In each chapter we'll discuss a slew of related problems (often as anecdotes), then move on to discuss a group of solutions relevant to the overall topic. To fully absorb everything you may need to lengthen your attention span to cover multiple pages, engage your right brain to make connections, or just plain sleep on it!

We should also make a couple more disclaimers. As we like to joke in our talks, "These opinions are purely our own and are based on our experiences. If you disagree, you're welcome to get your own talk." Just as with our oral presentations, we encourage any and all discussion that arises from the topics in this book. We're happy to chat about feedback, corrections, new opinions, and disagreements: you can find us at *http://www.debuggingteams.com/*. Everything in this book comes from our own trials by fire and the lessons that came out of our numerous mistakes.

You should also know that every name used in our examples has been changed to protect the innocent (or guilty).

THE CONTENTS OF THIS BOOK ARE NOT TAUGHT IN SCHOOL

Most of the software engineers we know have spent anywhere from 4 to 10 years in school learning about computer science and software engineering. And yet there are hardly any curricula[1] that actually teach you how to communicate and collaborate in a team or a company. Sure, most students are required to participate in a group project at some point in their academic career, but there's a big difference between teaching someone how to successfully work with another person and throwing him into a situation of forced collaboration. Most students end up jaded by the experience.

---

1 We've read *PeopleWare* by Tom DeMarco, and it's a great book, but it's not so much a book for individual contributors to learn how to work more efficiently with humans as it is a book for managers to learn how to make teams more successful.

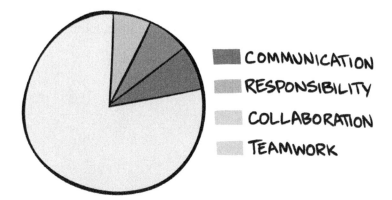

WHAT GROUP PROJECTS ARE SUPPOSED TO TEACH YOU

- COMMUNICATION
- RESPONSIBILITY
- COLLABORATION
- TEAMWORK

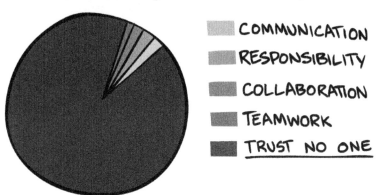

WHAT GROUP PROJECTS ACTUALLY TEACH YOU

- COMMUNICATION
- RESPONSIBILITY
- COLLABORATION
- TEAMWORK
- TRUST NO ONE

endlessorigami.com

The Pitch

Being a successful programmer isn't just about learning the latest languages or writing the fastest code. Professional coders almost always work in teams, and it turns out that one's team *directly* affects that individual's productivity and happiness more than many people would like to admit.

The basic idea of this book is simple: writing software is a team sport, and we posit that the human factors involved have as much influence on the outcome as the technical factors. Even if they've spent decades learning the technical side of programming, most people haven't really focused on the human component. Learning to collaborate is just as important to success. If you invest in the "soft skills" of engineering, you can have a much greater impact for the same amount of effort.

The Myth of the Genius Programmer

Since this is a book about the social perils of creative development, it makes sense to focus on the one variable you definitely have control of: you.

People are inherently imperfect. But before you can understand the bugs in your coworkers, you need to understand the bugs in yourself. We're going to ask you to think about your own reactions, behaviors, and attitudes—and in return, we hope you gain some real insight into how to become a more efficient and successful software engineer. You'll end up spending less energy dealing with people-related problems and more time writing great code.

The critical idea in this chapter is to understand that software development is a team sport. And in order to succeed on an engineering team—or in any other creative collaboration—you need to reorganize your behaviors around the core principles of humility, respect, and trust.

Before we get ahead of ourselves, let's start by observing how programmers behave in general.

Help Me Hide My Code

The two of us have been speaking at programming conferences quite a bit for the past ten years. After launching Google's open source Project Hosting service back in 2006, we used to get lots of questions and requests about the product. Back in mid-2008, we noticed a distinctive trend in the sort of requests we were getting:

Can you guys please give Subversion on Google Code the ability to hide specific branches?

Can you guys make it possible to create open source projects that start out hidden to the world, then get revealed when they're ready?

Hi, I want to rewrite all my code from scratch, can you please wipe all the history?

Can you spot a common theme to these requests?

The answer is *insecurity*. People are afraid of others seeing and judging their work in progress. In one sense, it's just a part of human nature—nobody likes to be criticized, especially for things that aren't finished. This attitude tipped us off to a trend within software development. Insecurity is actually the symptom of a larger problem.

The Genius Myth

The two of us lived in Chicago throughout the 1990s and got to witness the amazing run of championship wins by the Chicago Bulls. The national media was saturated for years with stories about this amazing basketball team. But what did TV and newspapers really focus on? Not so much the team, but Michael Jordan, the superstar. Every player around the world wanted to *be* MJ. We watched him dance circles around other players. We watched him in television commercials. We went to see silly movies where he played basketball with cartoon characters. He was a star, and every kid on every court practicing hoops secretly wished to grow up and follow his path.

Programmers have that same instinct—to find idols and worship them. Linus Torvalds, Richard Stallman, Bill Gates—all heroes who changed the world with heroic feats. Linus wrote Linux by himself, right?

Actually, Linus just wrote the beginnings of a proof-of-concept Unix-like kernel, and showed it to an email list. That was no small task, and it was definitely an impressive achievement, but it was just the tip of the iceberg. Linux is hundreds of times bigger than that and was developed by hundreds of smart people. Linus's real achievement was to *lead* these people and coordinate their work; Linux is the shining result of their collective labor. (And Unix itself was written by a group of smart people at Bell Labs, not entirely by Ken Thompson and Dennis Ritchie.)

On that same note, did Stallman personally write all of the Free Software Foundation's software? He wrote the first generation of Emacs. But hundreds of others were responsible for bash, the GCC tool chain, and all the rest of the software that runs on Linux. Steve Jobs led an entire team that built the Macintosh, and while Bill Gates is known for writing a BASIC interpreter for early home computers, his bigger achievement was building a successful company around MS-DOS. Yet they all became leaders and symbols of their collective achievements.

And how about Michael Jordan?

It's the same story. We idolize him, but the fact is that he didn't win every basketball game by himself. His true genius was in the way he worked *with* his team. The team's coach, Phil Jackson, was extremely clever—his coaching techniques are legendary: he recognized that one player alone never wins a championship and so he assembled an entire "dream team" around MJ. The team was a well-oiled machine—at least as impressive as Michael himself.

So why do we repeatedly idolize the individual in these stories? Why do people buy products endorsed by celebrities? Why do we want to buy Michelle Obama's dress or Michael Jordan's shoes?

Celebrity is a big part of it. Humans have a natural instinct to locate leaders and role models, idolize them, and attempt to imitate them. We all need heroes for inspiration, and the programming world has its heroes too. The phenomenon of "techie-celebrity" has almost spilled over into mythology. We all want to write something world-changing like Linux or design the next brilliant programming language.

Deep down we all secretly wish to be geniuses. The ultimate geek fantasy is to be struck by an awesome new concept. You go into your Batcave for weeks or months, slaving away at a perfect implementation of your idea. You then "unleash" your software on the world, shocking everyone with your genius. Your peers are astonished by your cleverness. People line up to use your software. Fame and fortune follow naturally.

But hold on: time for a reality check. You're probably not a genius.

No offense, of course—we're sure you're a very intelligent guy or gal. But do you realize how rare *actual* geniuses really are? Sure, you write code, and that's a tricky skill that probably puts you in a bracket above a lot of the human population. But even if you are a genius, it turns out that *that's not enough*. Geniuses still make mistakes, and having brilliant ideas and elite programming skills doesn't guarantee that your software will be a hit. What's going to make or break your career is how well you collaborate with others.

It turns out that this Genius Myth is just another aspect of our insecurity. Most programmers are afraid to share work they've only just started, because it means peers will see their mistakes and know the author of the code is *not a genius*. To quote a programmer from Ben's blog:

*I know I get SERIOUSLY insecure about people looking before something
is done. Like they are going to seriously judge me and think I'm an idiot.*

This is an extremely common feeling among programmers, and the natural
reaction is to hide in a cave and work, work, work. Nobody will see your goof-ups;
you still have a chance to unveil your masterpiece when you're done. Hide away
until all of it is perfect.

Another common motivation for holding your cards close to your chest is the
fear that another programmer might take your idea and run with it before you
get around to working on it. By keeping it secret, you control the idea.

We know what you're probably thinking now: so what? Shouldn't people be
allowed to work however they want?

Actually, no. In this case we assert that you're doing it wrong, and it *is* a big
deal. Here's why.

Hiding Is Considered Harmful

If you spend all your time working alone, you're *increasing* the risk of failure and
cheating your potential for growth.

First of all, how do you even know if you're on the right track?

Imagine you're a bicycle-design enthusiast, and one day you get a brilliant
idea for a completely new way to design a gear shifter. You order parts and proceed to spend weeks holed up in your garage trying to build a prototype. When
your neighbor—also a bike advocate—asks you what's up, you decide not to talk
about it. You don't want anyone to know about your project until it's absolutely
perfect. Another few months go by and you're having trouble making your prototype work correctly. But because you're working in secrecy, it's impossible to
solicit advice from your mechanically inclined friends.

Then one day your neighbor pulls his bike out of his garage with a radical
new gear-shifting mechanism. Turns out he's been building something very similar to your invention, but with the help of some friends down at the bike shop.
At this point you're exasperated. You show him your work. He points out that
your design had some simple flaws—ones that might have been fixed in the first
week if you had shown him.

There are a number of lessons to learn here. If you keep your great idea hidden from the world and refuse to show anyone anything until the implementation is polished, you're taking a huge gamble. It's easy to make fundamental design mistakes early on. You risk reinventing wheels.[1] And you forfeit the benefits of collaboration too: notice how much faster your neighbor moved by working with others? This is why people dip their toes in the water before jumping in the deep end: you need to make sure that you're working on the right thing, you're doing it correctly, and it hasn't been done before. The chances of an early misstep are high. The more feedback you solicit early on, the more you lower this risk.[2] Remember the tried-and-true mantra of "Fail early, fail fast, fail often"— we'll discuss the importance of failure at length later in the book.

Early sharing isn't just about preventing personal missteps and getting your ideas vetted. It's also important to strengthen what we call the *bus factor* of your project.

Bus factor (noun): the number of people that need to get hit by a bus before your project is completely doomed.

---

1 Literally, if you are, in fact, a bike designer.

2 We should note that sometimes it's dangerous to get too much feedback too early in the process, but we'll cover that in a later chapter.

How dispersed is the knowledge and know-how in your project? If you're the only person who understands how the prototype code works, it may be nice job security, but it also means the project is toast if you get hit by a bus. If you're working with a friend, however, you've doubled the bus factor. And if you've got a small team designing and prototyping together, things are even better—the project won't be over when a team member disappears. Remember: team members may not literally get hit by buses, but other unpredictable life events still happen. Someone may get married, have to move away, leave the company, or have to take care of a sick relative. You need to future-proof a project's success by managing the bus factor.

Beyond the bus factor, there's the issue of overall pace of progress. It's easy to forget that working alone is often a tough slog, much slower than people want to admit. How much do you learn when working alone? How fast do you move? The Web is a great dumping ground of opinions and information, but it's no substitute for actual human experience. Working with other people directly increases the collective wisdom behind the effort. When you get stuck on something absurd, how much time do you waste pulling yourself out of the hole? Think about how different the experience would be if you had a couple of peers to look over your shoulder and tell you—instantly—how you goofed and how to get past the problem. This is exactly why teams sit together (or do pair programming) in software engineering companies: you often find yourself needing a second pair of eyes.

Here's another analogy. Think about how you work with your compiler. When you sit down to write a large piece of software, do you spend days writing 10,000 lines of code, then when you think it's all done and completely perfect, press the "compile" button for the very first time? Of course you don't. Can you imagine what sort of disaster would result? As programmers we work best in *tight* feedback loops. Write a new function, compile. Add a test, compile. Refactor some code, compile. We get the typos and bugs fixed as soon as possible after generating code. We want the compiler at our side for every little step, playing wingman; some environments can even compile our code *as we type*. This is how we keep code quality high and make sure our software is evolving correctly bit by bit.

The same sort of rapid feedback loop is needed not just at the code level, but at the whole-project level too. Ambitious projects evolve quickly and have to adapt to changing environments as they go. Projects run into unpredictable design obstacles or political hazards, or we simply discover that things aren't working as planned. Requirements morph unexpectedly. How do you get that feedback loop so that you know the instant your plans or designs need to change? Answer: by working in a team. Eric Raymond is often quoted as saying, "Many eyes make all bugs shallow," but a better version might be, "Many eyes make sure your project stays relevant and on track." People working in caves awake to discover that while their original vision may be complete, the world has changed and made the product irrelevant.

Engineers and Offices

Twenty years ago conventional wisdom stated that for an engineer to be productive, she needed to have her own office with a door that closed. This was supposedly the only way she could have big uninterrupted slabs of time to deeply concentrate on writing reams of code.

We think that it's not only unnecessary for most engineers[3] to be in a private office, it's dangerous. Software today is written by teams, not individuals, and a high-bandwidth, readily available connection to the rest of your team is even more valuable than your Internet connection.

---

3 We do, however, acknowledge that serious introverts likely need more peace, quiet, and alone time than most people and may benefit from a more quiet environment if not their own office.

You can have all the uninterrupted time in the world, but if you're using it to work on *the wrong thing*, you're wasting your time.

Unfortunately, it seems that modern-day tech companies have swung the pendulum to the exact opposite extreme. Walk into their offices and you'll often find engineers clustered together in massive rooms—50 or 100 people together—with no walls whatsoever. This "open floor plan" is now a topic of huge debate. The tiniest conversation becomes public, and people end up not talking for risk of annoying dozens of neighbors. This is just as bad as private offices!

We think the middle ground is really the best solution. Group teams of 6 to 12 people together in small rooms (or large offices), so as to make it easy (and nonembarrassing) for spontaneous conversation to happen.

Of course, in any situation, individual engineers still need a way to filter out noise and interruptions, which is why most teams we've seen have developed a way to communicate that they're currently busy and that you should limit interruptions. We used to work on a team with a vocal interrupt protocol: if you wanted to talk, you would say "breakpoint *Mary*," where *Mary* was the name of the person you wanted to talk to. If Mary was at a point where she could stop, she would swing her chair around and listen. If Mary was too busy, she'd just say "ack" and you'd go on with other things until she finished with her current head state.

Other teams give out noise-canceling headphones to engineers to make it easier to deal with background noise—in fact, in many companies the very act of wearing headphones is a common signal that means "don't disturb me unless it's really important." Still other teams have tokens or stuffed animals that team members put on their monitor to signify that they should be interrupted only in case of emergency.

Don't misunderstand us—we still think engineers need uninterrupted time to focus on writing code, but we think they need a high-bandwidth, low-friction connection to their team just as much. Finding the right balance is an art.

So what it boils down to is this: *working alone is inherently riskier than working with others.* While you may be afraid of someone stealing your idea or thinking you're dumb, you should be much more scared of wasting huge swaths of your time toiling away on the wrong thing.

Sadly, this problem of "clutching ideas to the chest" isn't unique to software engineering—it's a pervasive problem across all fields. For example, professional science is *supposed* to be about the free and open exchange of information. But the desperate need to "publish or perish" and to compete for grants has had exactly the opposite effect. Great thinkers don't share ideas. They cling to them obsessively, do their research in private, hide all mistakes along the path, and then ultimately publish a paper, making it sound like the whole process was effortless and obvious. And the results are often disastrous: they accidentally duplicated someone else's work, or they made an undetected mistake early on, or they produced something that used to be interesting but is now regarded as useless. The amount of wasted time and effort is tragic.

Don't become another statistic.

It's All About the Team

So let's back up now and put all these ideas together.

The point we've been hammering is that in the realm of programming, lone craftsmen are extremely rare—and even when they do exist, they don't perform superhuman achievements in a vacuum; their world-changing accomplishment is almost always the result of a spark of inspiration followed by a heroic team effort.

Creating a superstar *team* is the real goal, and is fiendishly difficult. The best teams make brilliant use of their superstars, but the whole is always greater than the sum of its parts.

Let's put this idea into simpler words:

Software development is a team sport.

This may be a difficult concept at first, since it directly contradicts our inner Genius Programmer fantasy. Try chanting it as a mantra.

It's not enough to be brilliant when you're alone in your hacker's lair. You're not going to change the world or delight millions of computer users by hiding and preparing your secret invention. You need to *work* with other people. Share your vision. Divide the labor. Learn from others. Create a brilliant team.

Consider this: how many pieces of widely used, successful software can you name that were truly written by a *single* person? (Some people might say "LaTeX," but it's hardly "widely used," unless you consider the number of people writing scientific papers to be a statistically significant portion of all computer users!)

We're going to repeat this team-sport concept over and over throughout the book. High-functioning teams are gold and the true key to success. You should be aiming for this experience however you can; that's what this book is all about.

The Three Pillars

So the point about working in teams has been made. If teamwork is the best route to producing great software, how does one build (or find) a great team?

It's not quite that simple. In order to reach collaborative nirvana, you first need to learn and embrace what we call the "three pillars" of social skills. These three principles aren't just about greasing the wheels of relationships; they're the foundation on which all healthy interaction and collaboration are based.

Humility

You are not the center of the universe. You're neither omniscient nor infallible. You're open to self-improvement.

Respect

You genuinely care about others you work with. You treat them as human beings, and appreciate their abilities and accomplishments.

Trust

You believe others are competent and will do the right thing, and you're OK with letting them drive when appropriate.[4]

Together, we refer to these principles as HRT. We pronounce this as "heart" and not "hurt" because it's all about *decreasing* pain and not about injuring people. In fact, our main thesis is built directly on these pillars:

Almost every social conflict can ultimately be traced back to a lack of humility, respect, or trust.

It may sound implausible at first, but give it a try. Think about some nasty or uncomfortable social situation in your life right now. At the basest level, is everyone being appropriately humble? Are people really respecting one another? Is there mutual trust?

We believe these principles are so important that we've even structured this book around them.

This book begins with you: getting you to embrace HRT and really internalize what it means to put HRT at the center of your interactions. That's what this first chapter is about. From there we create ever-expanding circles of influence.

In Chapter 2 we discuss the challenge of building a team based on the three pillars. Creating a team culture is the critical next step to success—this is the "dream team" discussed earlier.

We then examine people who are interacting with your team on a daily basis, but may not be part of the core team culture. These may be coworkers from other teams, or just volunteers offering to help on your project. Many of them not only disregard HRT, but they can be downright poisonous! Learning to defend your team from them is the first order of business. Removing their fangs and sucking

---

4 This is incredibly difficult if you've been burned in the past by delegating to incompetent people.

them into your culture should be the ultimate goal, however. It's a great way to expand a team.

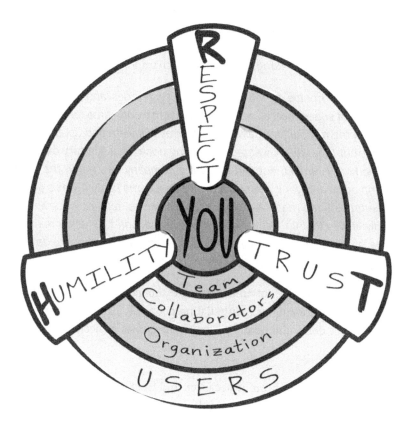

Most teams work within a larger company, and this environment can often be just as much of an impediment as poisonous people. Learning how to navigate these organizational obstacles can be the difference between launching a product and getting that very same product canceled.

Finally, we consider the users of your software. Sometimes we forget they exist, but they are the lifeblood of your project. Without users, your software has no purpose. The same HRT principles that thrive in your team can and should be applied to the way you interact with your users, and the benefits reaped are tremendous.

Let's pause for a moment.

When you picked up this book, you probably weren't thinking you were signing up for some sort of weekly support group. We empathize. Dealing with social problems can be difficult. People are messy, unpredictable, and often annoying to interface with. Rather than putting energy into analyzing social situations and making strategic moves, it's tempting to write off the whole effort. It's much easier to hang out with a predictable compiler, isn't it? Why bother with the social stuff at all?

Here's a quote from a famous lecture by Richard Hamming:[5]

> By taking the trouble to tell jokes to the secretaries and being a little friendly, I got superb secretarial help. For instance, one time for some idiot reason all the reproducing services at Murray Hill were tied up. Don't ask me how, but they were. I wanted something done. My secretary called up somebody at Holmdel, hopped [into] the company car, made the hour-long trip down and got it reproduced, and then came back. It was a payoff for the times I had made an effort to cheer her up, tell her jokes and be friendly; it was that little extra work that later paid off for me. By realizing you have to use the system and studying how to get the system to do your work, you learn how to adapt the system to your desires.

The moral is this: do not underestimate the power of playing the social game. It's not about tricking or manipulating people; it's about creating relationships to get things done, and relationships *always* outlast projects.

HRT in Practice

All of this preaching about humility, respect, and trust sounds like sermon material. Let's come out of the clouds and think about how to apply these ideas in real-life situations. We're looking for practical suggestions and so we're going to examine a list of specific behaviors and examples you can start with. Many of them may sound obvious at first, but once you start thinking about them you'll notice how often you (and your peers) are guilty of *not* following them.

---

5 "You and Your Research," *http://bit.ly/hamming_paper*

LOSE THE EGO

OK, this is sort of a simpler way of telling someone without enough *humility* to lose his 'tude. Nobody wants to work with someone who consistently behaves like he's the most important person in the room. Even if you know you're the wisest person in the discussion, don't wave it in people's faces. For example, do you always feel like you need to have the first or last word on every subject? Do you feel the need to comment on every detail in a proposal or discussion? Or do you know somebody who does these things?

Note that "being humble" is *not* the same as saying one should be an utter doormat: there's nothing wrong with self-confidence. Just don't come off like a know-it-all. Even better, think about going for a "collective" ego instead; rather than worrying about whether you're personally awesome, try to build a sense of team accomplishment and group pride. For example, the Apache Software Foundation has a long history of creating communities around software projects; these communities have incredibly strong identities and reject people who are more concerned about self-promotion.

Ego manifests itself in many ways, and a lot of the time it can get in the way of your productivity and slow you down. Here's another great story from Hamming's lecture that illustrates this point perfectly:

> John Tukey almost always dressed very casually. He would go into an important office and it would take a long time before the other fellow realized that this is a first-class man and he had better listen. For a long time John has had to overcome this kind of hostility. It's wasted effort! I didn't say you should conform; I said, "The appearance of conforming gets you a long way." If you chose to assert your ego in any number of ways, "I am going to do it my way," you pay a small steady price throughout the whole of your professional career. And this, over a whole lifetime, adds up to an enormous amount of needless trouble. [...] By realizing you have to use the system and studying how to get the system to do your work, you learn how to adapt the system to your desires. Or you can fight it steadily, as a small, undeclared war, for the whole of your life.

LEARN TO BOTH DEAL OUT AND HANDLE CRITICISM

Joe started a new job as a programmer. After his first week he really started digging into the code base. Because he cared about what was going on, he started gently questioning other teammates about their contributions. He sent simple code reviews by email, politely asking about design assumptions or pointing out places where logic could be improved. After a couple of weeks he was summoned to his director's office. "What's the problem?" Joe asked. "Did I do something wrong?" The director looked concerned: "We've had a lot of complaints about your behavior, Joe. Apparently you've been really harsh toward your teammates, criticizing them left and right. They're upset. You need to tone it down." Joe was utterly baffled. In a strong culture based on HRT, Joe's code reviews should have been welcomed and appreciated by his peers. In this case, however, Joe should have been more sensitive to the team's widespread insecurity and should have used subtler means to introduce code reviews into the culture.

Criticism is almost never personal in a professional software engineering environment—it's usually just part of the process of making a better product. The trick is to make sure you (and those around you) understand the difference between constructive criticism of someone's creative output and flat-out assaults against someone's character. The latter is useless—it's petty and nearly impossible to act on. The former is always helpful and gives guidance on how to improve. And most importantly, it's imbued with *respect*: the person giving the constructive criticism genuinely cares about the other person and wants her to improve herself or her work. Learn to respect your peers and give constructive criticism politely. If you truly respect someone, you'll be motivated to choose tactful, helpful phrasing—a skill acquired with much practice.

On the other side of the conversation, you need to learn to accept criticism as well. This means not just being *humble* about your skills, but *trusting* that the other person has your best interests (and those of your project!) at heart and doesn't actually think you're an idiot. Programming is a skill like anything else. It improves with practice. If a peer pointed out ways in which you could improve your juggling, would you take it as an attack on your character and value as a human being? We hope not. In the same way, *your self-worth shouldn't be connected to the code you write—or any creative project you build*. To repeat ourselves: you are not your code. Say that over and over. *You are not what you make.* You need to not only believe it yourself, but get your coworkers to believe it too.

For example, if you have an insecure collaborator, here's what *not* to say: "Man, you totally got the control flow wrong on that method there. You should be using the standard xyzzy code pattern like everyone else." This feedback is full of antipatterns: you're telling someone he's "wrong" (as if the world were black and white!), demanding he change something, and accusing him of creating something that goes against what everyone else is doing (making him feel stupid). The response is going to be overly emotional, coming from someone put on the defense.

A better way to say the same thing might be, "Hey, I'm confused by the control flow in this section here. I wonder if the xyzzy code pattern might make this clearer and easier to maintain?" Notice how you're using humility to make the question about you, not him. He's not wrong; you're just having trouble understanding the code. The suggestion is merely offered up as a way to clarify things for poor little you, and possibly helping the project's long-term sustainability goals. You're also not demanding anything—you're giving your collaborator the ability to peacefully reject the suggestion. The discussion stays in the realm of the code itself and isn't about anyone's value or coding skills.

FAIL FAST AND ITERATE

There's a well-known (and clichéd) urban legend in the business world about a manager who makes a mistake and loses an impressive $10 million. He dejectedly goes into the office the next day and starts packing up his desk, and when he gets the inevitable "the CEO wants to see you in his office" call, he trudges into the CEO's office and quietly slides a piece of paper across the desk to the CEO.

"What's this?" asks the CEO.

"My resignation," says the exec. "I assume you called me in here to fire me."

"*Fire* you?" responds the CEO, incredulously. "Why would I fire you? I just spent $10 million *training* you!"[6]

It's an extreme story, to be sure, but the CEO in this story understands that firing the exec wouldn't undo the $10 million loss, and it would compound it by losing a valuable executive who you can be damned sure won't make that kind of mistake again.

At Google, one of our favorite mottoes is "Failure is an option." It's widely recognized that if you're not failing now and then, you're not being innovative enough or taking enough risks. Failure is viewed as a golden opportunity to learn and improve for the next go-around. In fact, Thomas Edison is often quoted as saying, "If I find 10,000 ways something won't work, I haven't failed. I am not discouraged, because every wrong attempt discarded is another step forward."

Over in Google X—the division that works on "moonshots" like Google Glass and self-driving cars—failure is deliberately built into their incentive system. People come up with crazy ideas and coworkers are actively encouraged to shoot them down as fast as possible. Individuals are rewarded (and even compete!) to see how many ideas they can disprove or invalidate in a fixed period of time. When a concept is truly unable to be debunked at a whiteboard by all peers, only *then* does it proceed to early prototype.

The key to learning from your mistakes is to document your failures. Write up "postmortems," as they're often called in our business. Take extra care to make sure the postmortem document isn't just a useless list of apologies or excuses—that's not its purpose. A proper postmortem should always contain an explanation of *what was learned* and *what is going to change* as a result of the learning experience. Then make sure you put it in an easy-to-find place and really follow through on the proposed changes. Remember that properly documenting failures also makes it easier for other people (present and future) to know what happened and avoid repeating history. Don't erase your tracks—light them up like a runway for those who follow you!

---

6 A dozen variants of this legend can be found on the Web, attributed to different famous managers.

A good postmortem should include the following:

- A brief summary
- A timeline of the event, from discovery through investigation to resolution
- The primary cause of the event
- Impact and damage assessment
- A set of action items to fix the problem immediately
- A set of action items to prevent the event from happening again
- Lessons learned

LEAVE TIME FOR LEARNING

Cindy was a superstar—a software engineer who had truly mastered her specialized area. She was promoted to technical lead, saw her responsibilities increase, and rose to the challenge. Before long, she was mentoring everyone around her and teaching them the ropes. She was speaking at conferences on her subject and pretty soon ended up in charge of multiple teams. She absolutely loved being the "expert" all the time. And yet, she started to get bored. Somewhere along the way she stopped learning new things. The novelty of being the wisest, most experienced expert in the room started to wear thin. Despite all of the outward signs of mastery and success, something was missing. One day she got to work and realized that her chosen field simply wasn't so relevant anymore; people had moved on to other topics of interest. Where did she go wrong?

Let's face it: it is *fun* to be the most knowledgeable person in the room, and mentoring others can be incredibly rewarding. The problem is that once you reach a local maximum on your team, you stop learning. And when you stop learning, you get bored. Or accidentally become obsolete. It's really easy to get addicted to being a leading player; but only by giving up some ego will you ever change directions and get exposed to new things. Again, it's about increasing *humility* and being willing to learn as much as teach. Put yourself outside your comfort zone now and then; find a fishbowl with bigger fish than you and rise to whatever challenges they hand out to you. You'll be much happier in the long run.

LEARN PATIENCE

Years ago, Fitz was writing a tool to convert CVS repositories to Subversion (and later, Git), and, due to the vagaries of CVS, he kept unearthing bizarre bugs. Since his longtime friend and coworker Karl knew CVS quite intimately, he and Karl decided they should work together to fix these bugs.

A problem arose when they started pair programming together: Fitz was a bottom-up engineer who was content to dive into the muck and dig his way out by trying a lot of things quickly and skimming over the details. Karl, however, was a top-down engineer who wanted to get the full lay of the land and dive into the implementation of almost every method on the call stack before proceeding to tackle the bug. This resulted in some epic interpersonal conflicts, disagreements, and the occasional heated argument. It got to the point where the two of them simply couldn't pair-program together: it was too frustrating for both.

That said, the two of them had a longstanding history of trust and respect for each other. Combined with patience, this helped them work out a new method of collaborating. They would sit together at the computer, identify the bug, and split up and attack the problem from two directions at once (top-down and bottom-up), then come back together and meet in the middle with their findings. Their patience and willingness to improvise new working styles not only saved the project, but also saved the friendship.

BE OPEN TO INFLUENCE

The more you are open to influence, the more you are able to influence; the more vulnerable you are, the stronger you appear. These statements sound like bizarre contradictions. But everyone can think of someone they've worked with who is just maddeningly stubborn. No matter how much people try to persuade him, he digs his heels in even more. What eventually happens to such team members? In our experience, they end up just getting "routed around" like an obstacle everyone takes for granted. People stop listening to their opinions or objections. You certainly don't want that happening to you, so keep this idea in your head: it's OK for someone else to change your mind. Choose your battles carefully. Remember that in order to be heard properly, you first need to listen to others. In the case of being influenced, this listening should take place before you've put a stake in the ground or firmly declared that you've decided on something—if you're constantly changing your mind, people will think you're wishy-washy.

On the subject of vulnerability, this seems a bit strange at first too. If someone admitted she was ignorant of the topic at hand or didn't know how to solve a problem, what sort of credibility would she have in a group? Vulnerability is a show of weakness, and that destroys trust, right?

Not true. Admitting you've made a mistake or you're simply out of your league is a way to *increase* your status over the long run. In fact, it encompasses all of HRT: it's an outward show of *humility*, it's about accountability and taking responsibility, it's a signal that you *trust* others' opinions, and in return, people end up *respecting* your honesty and strength. Sometimes the best thing you can do is just say, "I don't know."

Consider professional politicians; they're notorious for never admitting error or ignorance, even when it's patently obvious that they're wrong or unknowledgeable about a subject. And for that reason most people don't believe a word that politicians say. This behavior exists primarily because politicians are constantly under attack by their opponents. When you're writing software, however, it's unnecessary to live in a constant state of defense—your teammates are collaborators, not competitors.

Next Steps

If you've made it this far, you're well on your way to mastering the art of "playing well with others." You've got to start with examining and meditating on your own behaviors. Once you've incorporated these strategies into your daily life, you'll find that collaboration will become much more natural and your engineering productivity will begin to noticeably increase.

The important changes begin with you and then spread outward to others. In the next chapter, we're going to talk about how to create a culture of HRT within your immediate team.

Building an Awesome Team Culture

Team cultures are incredibly varied and reflect a wide range of values and priorities. Some promote team success, and others promote team failure on a grand scale. However, even among the cultures that lead to successful teams, some are incredibly efficient and focus the majority of your team's effort on the work they set out to do, while others provide a great deal of distraction from the task at hand. In this chapter we'll talk about culture, with a strong focus on various communication techniques that contribute to success. We'll identify how these techniques can be used to create any product more efficiently with a team of humans.

What Is Culture?

When you hear the word *culture*, your thoughts typically wander to either an evening at the opera or the dish of jelly growing bacteria that you had back in high school biology. It turns out that engineering team culture isn't all that different from the latter.

If you've ever had a really delicious piece of sourdough bread and took the time to hunt down the person who baked it, you would find that the key ingredient to the bread is a starter containing yeast and lactobacillus bacteria living on a diet of flour and water. The yeast is what makes the bread rise, and the bacterium is what gives the bread that amazing tangy, sour flavor. However, not all lactobacillus strains are alike, and some create a more desirable flavor than others, so when a baker finds a starter (i.e., a bacteria culture/yeast mixture) that gives a really great sourdough flavor, she'll take care to maintain and grow the same bacterial culture by adding more flour and water to it. She'll then take small amounts of the starter and inoculate the ingredients for a loaf of bread, and *voilà*, she's got a great loaf of sourdough! This works because the culture in the starter not only creates the taste that she wants, but is strong enough to overtake any other wild strains of yeast or bacteria that might be in the bread ingredients or the air of the bakery.

Your team's culture is much like a good loaf of sourdough: your starter culture (your founders) inoculates your dough (your newcomers) with the culture, and as the yeast and bacteria (your team members) grow, out pops a great loaf of bread (your team). If your starter culture is strong, it's more than capable of overcoming any undesirable "wild strains" of culture that a newcomer might bring with him.[1] If your starter culture is weak, your team is vulnerable to unknown culture strains that newcomers might bring along. Unknown cultures bring with them unpredictable results, so it's better to begin with a known starter culture.

But a team's culture isn't just the way in which team members tackle their work, write code, or treat one another: it's a set of shared experiences, values, and goals that is unique to every engineering team we've ever been on or observed. The founding members of a team or company define the biggest part of a team's culture, but it will continue to change and develop over the life of the team.

The elements that make up a team culture vary wildly. Some are directly relevant to the *process* of doing work: in the case of writing software, you might set up code reviews and test-driven development, and place a high value on having good design docs before starting to crank out reams of code. Some elements might be more social, like going out to a particular restaurant for lunch every Thursday, or going out for drinks at a favorite bar on Fridays. Some of them might seem

---

1 Of course, a strong culture always has the option of incorporating any desirable "wild strains" that a newcomer brings in with her.

completely silly or outlandish to an outsider: the Google Pittsburgh engineering office used to be located next to a freight train track, and every time a train would come by (mind you, a very loud train), everyone would jump up and shoot Nerf darts at one another.[2] All of these things make up a team's culture and affect the team's productivity and ability to attract and retain good team members.

Take a look at any wildly successful software company today—Google, Apple, Microsoft, Oracle—and you'll find that each company has a very different culture: one that has its roots in the culture that was set by the founders and earliest employees. As these companies have grown and matured, their cultures have evolved and changed, but they've still retained a unique identity that trickles down to just about every aspect of how they develop products, treat their employees, and compete with other companies.

Why Should You Care?

In short, you should care because if you don't put effort into building and maintaining your culture, your team will eventually be overtaken by strong personalities that cultivate *their* culture in your team. This culture may turn out to be a productive, healthy culture that cranks out piles of great code, but more often than not, it won't turn out as such, and you'll suddenly find a lot of your energy that used to go into designing and creating your product is suddenly expended in arguments and infighting. Beyond that, it's important to have a culture that your team values and is willing to defend. If your team doesn't value your culture, not only is it difficult to build a strong team identity and collective pride in your work, but also it's very easy for a newcomer to change your culture into something that sucks.

The first mistake most team *members* make is to assume the team *leader* curates the culture of a team. Nothing could be further from the truth: while the founders and leads usually tend to the health of your culture, every member of your team participates in the culture and bears some responsibility for defining, maintaining, and defending the culture. When someone joins your team, she doesn't pick up the culture from the team leader alone, but from every team member she works with. For example, when you carefully review your new team member's work and explain to her why your team does something in a certain way, she'll quickly figure out what the team values in their product. She'll also

---

2 This scared the *hell* out of Fitz the first time he visited the Google Pittsburgh office.

learn about your culture from observing how the rest of your team works, inter-acts, and deals with conflict.

A "strong culture" is one that is open to change that improves it, yet is resist-ant to radical change that harms it. The team cultures that are most successful are those that focus the majority of the team's effort on shipping great software. If your team's primary focus is anything other than that (e.g., partying, attending meetings, practicing one-upmanship) your team may bond tightly, but you won't get very much software written. If you're happiest when writing code and ship-ping product, it's definitely in your best interest to find a team that values that, and to work to maintain that environment. It's not that you can't create some-thing great without a strong and productive culture, but it's going to cost you a lot more time and energy to do so without one. A strong culture gives you focus, efficiency, and strength, and these things make for a happier team.

The interesting thing about team culture is that, if you build a strongly defined one, it will become self-selecting. In the open source world, projects that are built on HRT and focused on writing clean, elegant, maintainable code will attract engineers who are interested in—surprise, surprise—working with people they respect and trust, and writing clean, elegant, maintainable code. If, however, your team is built on a culture of aggression, hazing, and ad hominem attacks, you're going to wind up attracting more people like that.

We've seen self-selecting cultures many times in the Apache Software Foun-dation: the ASF is a collection of software development teams that are community-based and that run on a consensus model. Many times a new con-tributor will join the mailing list and, through either ignorance or malice, will behave in a manner contrary to the team's culture. Community members will usually attempt to educate the newcomer (sometimes gently, sometimes, um, well, "not so gently"), and if the newcomer is not interested in how the ASF team does things, they'll usually head off in search of a more compatible project.

In the corporate world, teams self-select through the hiring process, whether implicitly in the skills and strengths that are valued in potential candidates, or explicitly by considering culture fit as part of the hiring process. Google takes the explicit approach in its hiring process as it looks specifically for culture fit when interviewing candidates: if Google interviews someone who in all respects looks like an outstanding engineer, but is incapable of working with a team of people or requires a very structured environment, the interviewers will raise a red flag in their feedback.

If you don't pay attention to culture fit as part of the hiring process and hire someone who isn't a fit, you'll wind up expending a tremendous amount of energy either getting the new hire to fit in or getting him to leave your team. Regardless of the result, the cost is high enough that it's definitely worthwhile to make sure new team members will work well with your existing team.

Interviewing for culture

The only way to make sure new team members will be a culture fit is to interview for it. Many companies (like Google) have culture fit as one of the criteria that interviewers look out for as they're speaking to a candidate. Some companies take it even further in their quest to avoid a hiring mistake: they have a separate interview for culture fit *before* doing the technical interviews because they don't want to even consider people who would fit technically but not culturally. This sort of process involvement is critical for creating and preserving a strong culture and it doesn't happen by accident; in fact, it is usually consciously created by the company's founders and early employees.

Culture and People

Creative work like writing software is different from simply knocking out widgets on an assembly line. Some types of work can be done with a few days of training and some basic tools, and if your worker quits and leaves (or doesn't work out), you just drop another worker in and on you go. In the assembly line environment, employees are accomplishing simple tasks, often by rote, with little creative-thinking or problem-solving skills required. In the software world, a great deal of creative thinking is required of engineers working on a product,[3] and if you want a great product, you need great engineers. If you want great engineers to do great work (and to stick around), you need to create a culture for them that allows them to safely share ideas and have a voice in the decision-making process.

If you want to get excellent engineers to work on your team, you need to start by hiring, well, some great engineers! That may sound weird, but the fact of the matter is that most great engineers want to be on teams with *other* great engineers. Many great engineers we know gravitate toward teams where they can

---

3 Some people think they can hire a whiz-bang architect and a bunch of mediocre programmers and create a good product. We think you can do that, but it's considerably less exciting and fun than working with a team of great people who inspire, challenge, and teach you.

learn from giants of the industry.[4] So how do you attract these engineers in the first place?

For starters, they're going to want to be able to not only contribute to the development of your product, but also participate in the product's decision-making process, and that usually means some level of consensus-driven management. In the case of top-down management, the alpha engineer is the team lead and lesser engineers are hired as team members. This is because subservient team members cost less and are easier to push around. And you're going to have a hard time finding great engineers to be on this team because, after all, what really great engineer wants to *ride* the bus when she can *drive* the bus at another company? But in the case of consensus-driven management, the entire team participates in the decision-making process.

Many people hear "consensus-based team" and immediately think of a bunch of hippies singing "Kumbaya" around a campfire and never making a decision or getting anything done, but that stereotype is symptomatic of a dysfunctional team much more than a consensus-based team. What we mean by "consensus" is that everyone has a strong sense of ownership and responsibility for the product's success and that the leaders really listen to the team (with an emphasis on the "respect" component of HRT). This may mean there are times when extended discussion and reflection is what the product needs to succeed, and there are other times when the team agrees they need to move quickly. In the latter case, team members may decide to entrust a great deal of the nitty-gritty day-to-day decision making to one or more team leads.[5] In order for this to happen, the team as a whole needs to agree on the general mission of the team, and believe it or not, the key to that is the development of a team mission statement (more on that later in this chapter).

Just as important as your team's decision-making process is the manner in which team members treat one another, because this is more self-selecting than anything else. If your team has a culture of chest thumping and yelling and screaming at one another, the only people you'll attract (and retain) are aggressive types who feel right at home in this environment composed of strong

---

4 Great engineers also demand great team leaders, because crappy leaders not only tend to be too insecure to deal with great engineers, but also tend to boss people around.

5 When consensus can't be reached, some teams have their leads decide, while other teams put it to a vote. The process your team uses is less important than having a process and sticking with it when there's conflict.

individual egos (in fact, most of the women we know find this kind of environment especially off-putting). If you create a culture of HRT where team members treat one another kindly and take the effort to give constructive criticism, you'll not only attract a much larger set of people, but you'll also spend a great deal more of your energy writing software. Having a strong team ego[6] is good; a team totally eclipsed by *individual* egos is a recipe for disaster. We'll discuss how to prevent this sort of situation in Chapter 4.

Constructive criticism is essential to the growth and development of any person or team, but many people will go to great lengths to avoid soliciting criticism. In some cases this is due to insecurity, but in most cases that we've seen it is because a person thinks that they are required to take action on any criticism received, even if they disagree with it. The best part about getting good constructive criticism is that you can pick and choose which pieces you want to act on. Let's say, for example, that you're getting ready for an important job interview and put on your favorite suit. You approach a trusted friend and ask how you look. If they say, "You've got spinach in your teeth, and I really hate your suit" you can take a quick floss break, but you don't *have* to change clothes as well. Criticism is a gift that you can either accept or reject.

If you're interested in improving your work or fixing your own personal bugs, these very friends and colleagues are the ones that can make you aware of things you do that might be hindering your effectiveness. Unless you have a truly remarkable level of self-awareness or introspection, without criticism, you'll just go on making the same mistakes no one wants to tell you about. For example, in the process of going to press with this book, we've had no fewer than a dozen people look at it and give us constructive criticism on our writing, and most of it was incredibly detailed and completely invaluable. Regardless of whether you think the book is good or bad, it would have been *considerably worse* if we had ignored this valuable feedback or been afraid to ask for it.

---

6 In other words, team pride.

It requires a certain amount of self-confidence to take any kind of criticism, and we think constructive criticism is the easiest kind to receive. On the downside, it's a lot harder to give someone constructive criticism than to simply lambast her or ridicule something she did. Of course, we realize it's incredibly difficult to solicit and then receive constructive criticism from most people—they assume that when you ask them to criticize your work, you're only looking for compliments and assurance. If you can find friends or colleagues who will constructively criticize your work when you ask them, hang on to these people because they're worth their weight in unobtainium.

Aggressive people can (usually) be productive in a quieter environment, but quieter, more introverted people rarely excel (or enjoy working) in an aggressive environment—it's not only harder to hear their voices over the noise, but it also tends to discourage them from being active participants.[7] If you're looking for a culture that allows the broadest range of people to work most efficiently, you should build that culture on humility, respect, and trust.

Calm, easygoing cultures built on respect are more vulnerable to disruption by aggressive people than aggressive cultures are vulnerable to disruption from more easygoing people. Easygoing cultures need to be aware of this and not let the aggressive newcomer take over, typically by refusing to engage this person in an aggressive tone. In some cases, one or more of the more senior team members may have to meet the aggressive newcomer head-on to prevent her from harming an easygoing team culture. Again, we'll talk a lot more about how to deal with these sorts of "poisonous people" in Chapter 4.

Communication Patterns of Successful Cultures

Communication can often be a challenge when you're working with a team, Communication can often be a challenge when working with a team, particularly for engineers, who would rather spend an afternoon with a (predictable, logical) compiler than spend three minutes with a (unpredictable, emotional) human being. In many cases, engineers see communication work as an obstacle to be overcome on the road to writing more code, but if your team isn't in agreement or is uninformed, there's no way to know if you're writing the right code in the first place.

---

7 See Susan Cain's excellent TED Talk, "The Power of Introverts" (*http://www.youtube.com/watch?v=c0KYU2jOTM4*), or her book, *Quiet: The Power of Introverts* (Crown).

If you examine any successful, efficient culture, you'll find high value placed on numerous channels of communication, such as mailing lists, design docs, chat rooms, mission statements, code comments, production how-tos, and more. It takes considerable effort to make sure everyone on a team agrees on the team's direction and understands exactly what the team needs to do. All this effort, however, is an investment that pays off in increased productivity and team happiness.

A good general rule around communication is to include as few people as necessary in *synchronous* communication (like meetings and phone calls), and to go for a broader audience in *asynchronous* communication (like email, issue trackers, and document comments). Synchronous communications have a high cost: they require that participants interrupt their workday and receive information on your schedule. Asynchronous communications, however, can be dealt with at a time and place most convenient for the recipient. Every time you interrupt someone's work it will take some amount of time for them to get back up to speed—always be conscious of when you're doing this.

But most importantly, you should make certain that all information is available to as many people as possible in your project's documentation. Let's cover the primary communication mechanisms that people use in the process of writing software with a team. Some of these may seem obvious, but there are many nuances that make them worth reviewing. One thing is certain: if you don't expend any effort on good communication, you'll waste considerable effort doing work that's either unnecessary or already being done by other members of your team.

High-Level Synchronization

At the highest level, the team needs to keep common goals in sync and follow best practices around communicating their progress.

THE MISSION STATEMENT—NO, REALLY

When you hear someone say "mission statement," the odds are good that the first thing that springs to mind are the insipid, overhyped, marketing-speak mission statements that are bandied about by a lot of big companies. An example is the following mission statement from a very large telecommunications company that will remain nameless:

> We aspire to be the most admired and valuable company in the world. Our goal is to enrich our customers' personal lives and to make their businesses more successful by bringing to market exciting and useful communications services, building shareowner value in the process.

Oddly enough, I've yet to meet *anyone* who admires that company! Here's another example from another major corporation:

> Providing solutions in real time to meet our customers' needs.

What does that even *mean?* It could mean absolutely anything at all—if we worked for that company, we wouldn't know if it was more important to wash the car, fix a leaky pipe, or deliver a pizza. It's this kind of corporate doublespeak that gives mission statements a bad name.

For an effective, efficient team, writing a mission statement is a way to concisely define the direction and limit the scope of your product. Writing a good mission statement takes some time and effort, but it can potentially save you *years* of work by clarifying what your team should and shouldn't[8] be working on.

When Google decided to move development of the Google Web Toolkit (GWT) to an open source project, we acted as the team mentors. We reviewed the

---

8 We can't stress enough how important this is—saying no to all of the distractions is what keeps you focused.

many differences between open and closed source development, paying specific attention to the difficulties of designing, discussing, and writing software in an environment where anyone can poke their nose in to offer an opinion, contribute a patch, or criticize the most minute aspect of your product.[9] After going over these challenges, we told the team they needed to come up with a mission statement as a way to describe to the public at large what their product goals (and nongoals!) were.

Some of the team members balked at this for many of the reasons outlined earlier, but others seemed curious, and the team lead seemed to think it was a great idea. However, when we sat down to start writing the mission statement, a lot of debate about the content, substance, and style of the mission statement ensued. After a great deal of discussion (and a few more meetings), the team came up not only with a great, concise mission statement, but also an entire document called "Making GWT Better"[10] explaining the statement phrase by phrase. They even included a section that described what the project's *nongoals* were. Here's the mission statement:

> GWT's mission is to radically improve the web experience for users by enabling developers to use existing Java tools to build no-compromise AJAX for any modern browser.

There's a ton of substance packed into that sentence, and we think it's an excellent example of a mission statement: it includes both a direction (improve the web experience...by enabling developers) and a scope limiter (Java tools). Several years later we were having dinner with the team lead, and Fitz told him how thankful we were that he had supported us so strongly in our effort to get the team to write a mission statement. He responded that he had actually thought the entire exercise was a waste of time when we first proposed it, but that once he started debating it with the team, he discovered something he'd never known: his lead engineers did not agree on the direction of the product!

In this case, writing a mission statement forced them to confront their differences and come to an agreement on their product's direction, a problem that could have slowed down (or stopped) development of the product as time went

---

9 We've often likened writing open source software to building card houses on a trampoline. It takes a steady hand, a lot of patience, and a willingness to deal with people who leap before looking.

10 "Making GWT Better" is located at *http://code.google.com/webtoolkit/makinggwtbetter.html* and is worth a read as a model mission statement document.

on. They posted their mission statement on the Web, and not only did the entire team have a laser focus on what they wanted to do with their product, but it saved them months of time arguing with potential contributors about the product's direction—they just pointed newcomers to "Making GWT Better" and most questions were answered.

As your project progresses, the mission statement keeps things on track. It shouldn't become an insurmountable impediment to change, however. If radical changes happen to the environment or business plan (say, at a startup company), software team members need to be honest with themselves and reevaluate whether the mission still makes sense. Changing a constitution is a deliberately difficult process, as it prevents people from doing so whimsically. But in dramatic times it's at least *possible* to change it and it should be considered. If a company or product pivots suddenly, the mission statement needs to keep up.

EFFICIENT MEETINGS

Most people would classify meetings as a necessary evil. While they can be highly effective when used skillfully, they're frequently abused, usually disorganized, and almost always too long. We like our meetings like we like our sewage treatment plants: few, far between, and downwind. So we'll keep this section brief and just cover team meetings.

Let's start with the most dreaded meeting of all: the standing meeting. This meeting usually takes place every week, and should absolutely be kept to basic announcements and introductions—going around the room for a status update from every attendee (whether they have something important to add or not) is a recipe for wasted time, rolling eyes, and a burning desire to punch yourself in the throat just to make it end.

Anything worth deeper discussion should take place after the meeting, with only the relevant people sticking around for it. This is also a great way to avoid derailing a meeting when someone starts to do a deep dive into a particular meeting topic: the person running the meeting should just add the topic to a list of "sidebars" and once the meeting is over, review them one at a time. If your team makes this a habit, it's easy to call "sidebar" on something that's getting off-track without putting anyone off. The key to making this meeting work is that people should be happy to leave the meeting once the main part of it is done, and if there's nothing that needs to be covered, or information that can be disseminated by email, don't hesitate to cancel the meeting. We've seen some cultures where meeting attendance is equated with status, so nobody wanted to be left out. Not to put too fine a point on it, but that is patently insane.

Daily standups

Some engineers swear by daily standups that are promoted by development methodologies like Agile, and these are acceptable if they are kept short and on point. These meetings usually start their lives short—15 minutes—with everyone actually standing up and giving a brief update on what they're working on, but without constant vigilance they tend to quickly turn into 30-minute-long sit-down meetings where people ramble on and on like they're in a group therapy session. If your team is going to have these meetings, *someone* needs to run them with authority and keep their growth in check.

If you're trying to design something new, try to include no more than five people in your meeting—it's practically impossible to come up with new designs and make decisions with more than five people in a room unless there's only one person in the room making the decisions. If you don't believe us, get five of your friends together, go downtown, and try to decide among the six of you how to do a walking tour that hits half a dozen tourist sites. The odds are good that you'll stand on the street corner arguing for most of the day unless you simply declare one person to be the final arbiter and then follow her wherever she goes.

Meetings are frequently an interruption to what many refer to as "make time," inspired by Paul Graham's "Maker's Schedule, Manager's Schedule."[11] It can be hard for anyone, especially engineers, to get into the zone if they're constantly stopping work to attend meetings. Schedule time on your calendar in three- to four-hour blocks and label these blocks as "busy" or even "make time," and get your work done. If you have to set up a meeting, try to set it up near another natural break in the day, like lunchtime, or at the very end of the day. At Google, there's a long (and unfortunately, often ignored) tradition of "No-meeting Thursdays"[12] in the interest of clearing time to just get work done. This is a good first step on the path to having 20 to 30 hours of make time set aside in larger blocks.

---

11 *http://www.paulgraham.com/makersschedule.html*

12 Google Engineering VP Wayne Rosing started this in 2001 in an attempt to improve the engineers' quality of life. Fitz blocked off his Thursdays for years, and it worked fairly well but required pretty rigorous monitoring and the occasional grumpy email when someone scheduled over it.

Note

Five simple rules for running a meeting:

1. Only invite people who absolutely need to be there.

2. Have an agenda and distribute it well before the meeting starts.

3. End the meeting early if you've accomplished the meeting's goals.

4. Keep the meeting on track.

5. Try to schedule the meeting near other interrupt points in your day (e.g., lunch, end of day).

If you're going to have a meeting, create an agenda and distribute it to all attendees at least a day before the meeting so that they'll know what to expect. Invite as few people as possible (remember the cost of synchronous communication). We know team members, managers, and even directors and VPs who will flat out ignore invitations to a meeting that has no agenda.

Only invite people to the meeting who actually need to be there for the meeting to accomplish its goal. Some people have taken to banning laptops in meetings after they've noticed attendees reading email instead of paying attention, but this is attacking the symptom and not the cause—people start reading email in a meeting because they probably *don't need to be in the meeting in the first place.*

Whoever's running the meeting should actually run the meeting and not hesitate to (gently) cut off someone who veers off-topic or, even worse, tries to monopolize the conversation. Doing this well can be tricky, but is worthwhile. And most importantly, don't be afraid to end a meeting early if you've completed the agenda.

WORKING IN A "GEOGRAPHICALLY CHALLENGED" TEAM

When you're part of a distributed team or working remotely from them, you not only need to find different ways to communicate, but also need to put more work into communication, period. If you're on a team that has remote workers, this means documenting and sharing decisions in writing, usually over email. Online chats, instant messages, and hallway conversations might be where a lot of discussion takes place, but there needs to be some way to broadcast relevant discussions like these to everyone to make sure they're informed and participating (and as a bonus, archived email lists provide documentation). Video chat is also incredibly useful as a quick conversation enabler, and besides, these days most laptops have built in webcams.

In the Subversion project we had a motto: "If the discussion didn't happen on the email list, then it never really happened." People spent lots of time bandying around ideas in chat rooms, but in order to make the resolutions "real" we had to be mindful of everyone else who didn't witness them. By forcing conversations to repost to email lists, we gave the entire distributed team a chance to see how decisions were arrived at (and to speak up if they wanted to). This is particularly critical if you're trying to encourage a consensus-based team culture.

Talking to someone from a remote location should be as frictionless as walking over to their desk. If you're working remotely, overcommunicate with your team using every available medium (e.g., online chat, instant messages, email, video chat, phone calls, etc.) to make sure everyone knows not only that you exist, but also what you're working on. And most important of all, *do not underestimate the bandwidth of a face-to-face conversation.*

Fitz once had an engineer who was working with a team in Colorado, and she was having trouble getting momentum on the project that she was sharing with them. She pulled Fitz aside to tell him this and he told her that she should hop on a flight to Colorado and spend a week with the team to kickstart their project. Two weeks later, she emailed Fitz from Colorado, after spending only a day there, with great news—not only had she gained great momentum on the project, but she was getting along great with the team after joining them for lunch and drinks after work.

Ben once had a team member, Corey, who started a new project with a team in another office. Corey was having a bit of a tough time getting traction with the new team and lamented this to Ben in their weekly one-on-one. Ben told Corey that he should fly out to the team's office and sit with them for a week to kick off the project. Corey was hesitant because of the cost of a flight and hotel, but he wasn't accounting for the *benefit* of the trip. Corey took a two-day trip to work with the team and he immediately realized how valuable it was to be there with the team. Not only did he gain the benefit of the additional bandwidth of in-person conversation, but, by having lunch together, and going out together after work one day, Corey and the team all got to know each other as *people*. As a result, future interactions with the team went much more smoothly, despite the fact that Corey was a thousand miles away.

Nothing replaces being in the same room

One thing to note about all of these people is that, despite all the advances in social media and videoconferencing technology, nothing even comes close to the bandwidth and the intimacy of being face to face with someone else in real life. If you're starting a new project or have an important meeting with someone in your company and you have the budget to be there in person, it's almost always worth the hassle of traveling. The impact of an in-person discussion etches itself into memory in ways that phone or video chats can't compete with.

A frequent argument against business travel is that it's too expensive or, in some cases, not affordable. While this may be the case for small geographically distributed companies, most large companies can afford this expense. The cost of not spending face time with your colleagues is higher than you think.

No matter how much you email, chat, or call, don't be afraid to regularly get on a plane and visit the rest of your team. This goes for remote employees, remote teams, and remote offices as well—make the time to get out to the home office and talk to people.

DESIGN DOCS

If you're an engineer, it's sometimes difficult to resist the urge to take a running leap into writing code for a new project, but this is rarely fruitful (unless you're throwing together a quick and dirty prototype). Just the same, many engineers rush right into coding before designing the software they intend to write, and this usually ends very badly.

A design doc is typically owned by one person, authored by two or three, and reviewed by a larger set. It serves not only as a high-level blueprint of your future project, but also as a low-cost way to communicate to your larger team what you want to do and how you intend to do it. Since you haven't spent weeks (or months) writing code, it's a lot easier to accept criticism at this point and you'll wind up with a better product and a better implementation. In addition, once you've nailed down the design doc, it will serve as your guide for both scheduling and dividing the work on your project. Once you start coding, however, you should treat your design doc as a living document and not one carved in stone: you and your team *should* update the document as your project grows and changes, not once you've shipped, although this is easier said than done. Most teams have no docs at all, while the rest have a short period of awesome docs, followed by a long period of out-of-date docs.

Having said that, make sure you don't take the "design doc religion" to the opposite extreme. We've seen control freaks write a four-page design essay for a program that's only 100 lines of code. If the project can be rewritten from scratch several times in the same amount of time it takes to write a design doc, a design doc is clearly a waste of time. Use experience and judgment when making these time calculations and trade-offs.

Day-to-Day Discussions

Assuming high-level goals are agreed upon, you need to worry about the tools your team uses for everyday coordination. These tools are useful, but they tend to have narrow communication bandwidth and, usually, a complete lack of metadata and secondary communication channels such as facial expressions and body language. As a result, they're more conducive to miscommunication and an inherent threat to HRT. Still, these tools are invaluable to most teams and (with a little effort) can give a good boost to productivity.

MAILING LISTS

We don't know of anyone who works with a team these days that doesn't use at least one mailing list, but there are a few things you can do with your mailing lists to make them more useful.

Many big successful projects have multiple mailing lists, separating development discussions, code reviews, user discussions, announcements, pager emails, and miscellaneous administrivia. Sometimes smaller projects attempt to emulate this as they're just getting started and create half a dozen mailing lists when they've only got three engineers and two users. This is the mailing list equivalent of providing six conference rooms for five people to carry on a discussion—you wind up with little coherence, a lot of echoes, and mostly empty rooms. It's really best to start with one list, and to add lists only when the amount of traffic on one list gets unmanageable (which is typically indicated by list members begging for mercy). An exception to that rule is to have automated emails and "bot" notifications go to their own list or at the very least use identifiers that make them easy to filter.

Take some time to establish proper etiquette around email discussions—keep discussions civil, and prevent filibustering by a "noisy minority."[13]

---

13 A "noisy minority" is usually characterized by one or two people who repeatedly respond to every single post in a thread, refuting every argument that doesn't align with theirs. A cursory examination of the thread in question might lead you to believe you've got a tremendous amount of dissent when, in fact, it's coming from just one or two disgruntled people. You need to address this behavior quickly and carefully (see Chapter 4 for more information on dealing with these sorts of people).

A mailing list isn't going to be your first choice for a discussion in a team that shares an office, but it's a good idea to send a copy of meeting agendas, meeting notes, decisions made, design docs, and any other relevant textual information to your team's mailing list so that you have a convenient central record. Set up these lists to archive all posts in a *searchable* index, either publicly available in the case of open source projects or on your company's intranet if you're working on a closed source project. Now you have a system of record for the history of your project, and it's easy to refer back to it when a newcomer asks about the reasoning behind one or more decisions that you made in the past. If you don't have these discussions archived somewhere, you'll find yourself repeating them again and again and again and again.

ONLINE CHAT

Online chat is an incredibly convenient way for teams to communicate, especially since it provides a way to send a quick request to a teammate without interrupting her work (providing, of course, she has her chat program configured to not interrupt her work!). It's a good tool for teams to use if they're moving quickly on a new project, doing some light work in the evening or on the weekend, or if one team member is out of the office for a day or two. One-on-one chat is useful and certainly has its place in team communication, but we strongly recommend that teams use some sort of group chat mechanism.[14]

Years before instant messaging became wildly popular, teams would hang out in an Internet Relay Chat (IRC) channel and most of their discussions would be in a group chat. This could be noisy at times, and it was easy enough for team members to break off to have a private chat if they were discussing something that was not of interest to the larger team, but in most cases discussions happened "in front of" the rest of the team. This allowed other people to join in on the conversation, lurk in the background and follow the discussion, or even catch up on discussions they missed earlier. This is convenient not only because of the ease with which ad hoc group discussions can start, but also because it helps to build community even in teams that are geographically dispersed. It's often surprising how much a newer team member can learn just by watching (or later reading) various discussions he's not necessarily participating in.

---

14 Of course, when an engineer needs uninterrupted time and can't afford the costs of context switching, it's totally acceptable to ignore chat.

With the advent of instant messaging, many of these conversations that would previously take place in the group chat room moved to private chat, which was the default for instant messenger. It's very tempting to indulge your insecurity and take what might be perceived as a stupid question to a one-on-one discussion rather than risk embarrassment in front of the rest of the team. Unfortunately, this increases the burden on the team because there's no shared lore created and different team members may ask other team members the same question over and over again.

Fortunately, group chat has seen a renaissance in 2014/2015 with the rise of Slack, a free (but not free software or open source) group messaging client that feels a lot like a modern-day IRC. Slack integrates with dozens of other products and has become the messaging tool of choice in smaller companies, startups, and even loosely connected groups of acquaintances on the Internet. While it still provides a means to send private messages, team owners get a weekly report telling them the percentage of private messages versus group messages. This makes it easy to give your team a gentle "push" to have more discussions in the group channels rather than one-on-one.

Regardless of the application you use for chat, we *strongly* recommend that your team have a convenient and accessible mechanism for group chat. It's well worth the effort in order to have this additional communication bandwidth in your team.

Group chat versus 1:1 instant messages

When many people first hear about IRC these days, they scoff at its primitive text-based environment because even the most modern of IRC clients tend to be less whizzy than outdated versions of iChat or Google Talk. Don't be fooled by the outdated look and feel of IRC—its killer features are that it was designed for multiperson chat and it's asynchronous; most clients keep an unlimited scroll-back record so that you can read back to see conversations among others that you missed. Slack is basically the modern-day version of IRC, and despite its whizzy integration of graphics, avatars, and emoji, at its heart it's still a text-based messaging system like IRC. It may be tempting to try out fancy videoconferencing packages, shared whiteboard systems, and more, but these systems often tend to be ineffective and can eliminate the asynchronous advantage of text-based group chat. If you're going to use something other than Slack or IRC, find something that is actually designed for group chat and isn't just an instant messaging system with group chat bolted on.

Sometimes people are more comfortable chatting online: we remember the first time we went to a hackathon where a number of open source contributors were going to meet (many for the first time) face to face and work on their projects together. We walked into an almost silent room to find a dozen tables—with six to eight people per table—furiously typing away at their laptops. We figured that, well, we were late, and everyone was already busy writing code, so we sat down, opened our laptops, fired up our editors, and signed on to the project's IRC channel to see if folks who couldn't make it to the hackathon were "virtually" there. We found a number of conversations taking place in the IRC channel. We said hello and mentioned that we'd just arrived at the hackathon room, and imagine our surprise when several people said hello in the IRC channel when they turned out to be sitting less than 10 feet away from us! Some of this was purely inertia as we were all used to chatting online, but in many cases it was just the most comfortable way for some people to communicate with the rest of the group. Fresh off a four-hour flight and desperate for some communication bandwidth, we got up and went from table to table to talk with people face to face.

There are no hard and fast rules for when to use chat versus email. Chat is more useful for fast-moving real-time discussions where a decision can be made easily and all participants are currently available. If some participants aren't around or the discussion is less pressing, email might be better. Just keep in mind the costs of synchronous versus asynchronous communication that we reviewed in "Communication Patterns of Successful Cultures" on page 31.

Using an Issue Tracker

If you're going to use an issue/bug tracker (and you should), it's important that you have some sort of process in place for processing and triaging bugs to encourage people to file and fix important bugs in a timely manner. If your bug tracker is neglected and not prioritized, people will stop filing bugs and begin shouting complaints into the void; and when your team eventually digs into the bug tracker, more than likely they will be fixing unimportant bugs and ignoring important ones.

Keep in mind that a bug tracker is really just a slightly specialized "Internet forum" or "bulletin board." As such, it shares most properties in common with email lists and the same best practices apply. Hallway conversations about bugs should be recorded as updates in the bug tracker, making thoughts and decisions "official" for all to see. Keep the tone civil and don't tolerate trollish behaviors.

We've also seen numerous occasions where a project manager is assigned the task of checking in on all open issues in the issue tracker. This can often not only create a great deal of churn, but also lead team members to start lengthy conversations in the issue tracker. If conversations get overly long or fragmented, take the discussion temporarily to the main email list—an email client is a much better tool for complex threads.

Communication as Part of Engineering

Hundreds and hundreds of books have been written about the software development process. While we're not going to dig into them all here, there are a few communication-related highlights that deserve mention, regardless of the development methodology you use. Even if you don't write software, there are a few lessons to be learned here—especially lessons about what *not* to do.

CODE COMMENTS

Code commenting style is very subjective. Verbose comments can often provide clues regarding the intent and reasoning of the original programmer and can be very useful, but at the cost of ongoing maintenance: out-of-date or incorrect comments drastically hinder understanding of a code base. Similarly, terse or non-existent comments can cause future maintainers or API consumers to waste time sleuthing. Comments are often used to point out missing structure and bad naming, and then go on to reexplain what the code already says. Comments should be focused on *why* the code is doing what it's doing, not *what* the code is doing.

Comments are most useful at the function or method level, especially as a means of documenting an API, and without going into exhaustive details, comments can be summed up with the popular Greek maxim, "μηδέν άγαν," or "nothing in excess." Beyond that, take the time to come up with a commenting style for your team and have everyone stick to it—we think being consistent is more important than the actual choice.[15] Your style guide should also explain the reason the guide exists and what it intends to prescribe—for example, here's the introduction to the Google C++ Style Guide:[16]

> C++ is the main development language used by many of Google's open-source projects. As every C++ programmer knows, the language has many powerful features, but this power brings with it complexity, which in turn can make code more bug-prone and harder to read and maintain.

---

15 See the excellent section on comments in *The Art of Readable Code* by Dustin Boswell and Trevor Foucher (O'Reilly).

16 Find this and several other style guides at *http://code.google.com/p/google-styleguide/*.

The goal of this guide is to manage this complexity by describing in detail the dos and don'ts of writing C++ code. These rules exist to keep the code base manageable while still allowing coders to use C++ language features productively.

Style, also known as readability, is what we call the conventions that govern our C++ code. The term Style is a bit of a misnomer, since these conventions cover far more than just source file formatting.

One way in which we keep the code base manageable is by enforcing consistency. It is very important that any programmer be able to look at another's code and quickly understand it. Maintaining a uniform style and following conventions means that we can more easily use "pattern-matching" to infer what various symbols are and what invariants are true about them. Creating common, required idioms and patterns makes code much easier to understand. In some cases there might be good arguments for changing certain style rules, but we nonetheless keep things as they are in order to preserve consistency.

Another issue this guide addresses is that of C++ feature bloat. C++ is a huge language with many advanced features. In some cases we constrain, or even ban, use of certain features. We do this to keep code simple and to avoid the various common errors and problems that these features can cause. This guide lists these features and explains why their use is restricted.

Open-source projects developed by Google conform to the requirements in this guide.

Note that this guide is not a C++ tutorial: we assume that the reader is familiar with the language.

Note that the guide doesn't make claims about enforcing the best or fastest way to write C++, but merely the importance of having consistency across the code base.

PUTTING YOUR NAME ON YOUR WORK

Everyone wants to get credit for work they do, from the artist who signs her painting to the author who puts her name on the spine of her book or the top of her blog. It's human nature to crave recognition in one way or another, but littering source files with your name is, in our opinion, more trouble than it's worth.

We've all seen these attributions at the top of source files, nestled snugly against the copyright declarations:

```
# ---------------------------------
# Created: October 1998 by Brian W. Fitzpatrick <fitz@red-bean.com>
# ---------------------------------
```

The tradition of putting your name at the top of your source code is an old one (heck, both of us have done it in the past), and may have been appropriate in an age where programs were written by individuals and not teams. Today, however, many people may touch a particular piece of code, and the issue of name attribution in a file is the cause of much discussion, wasted time, and hurt feelings. As a result, we advocate strongly against names as a sign of ownership in source code files (at best, include a name to designate a first choice to review any changes you might make to the file, but be careful that you don't imply ownership).

Let's imagine, for example, that you create a new file in your team's project—you write a few hundred lines of code, smack your name and the appropriate copyright header at the top of the file and send it off for code review, and later, commit it to the repository. No problems, no drama, no disagreements so far. Let's say that your teammate Adrian comes along and makes some changes to the file: at what point does he get to put his name at the top of the file? Does he have to fix a bug? Five bugs? Does he have to write a function? Two functions?

How many lines of code does he have to write? What if he writes a function, slaps his name on the file, and then someone else comes along and rewrites "his" function? Does this person now get to put her name on the file? Does she get to take Adrian's name off? Unlike other collaborative pieces of creative work—plays, novels, films—software keeps changing even after it's "done." So, while listing contributor credits at the end of a movie is a safe and static thing, attempting to add and remove names from a source file is a never-ending exercise in insanity.

Certainly you can answer all these questions and extensively document every possible edge case, but maintaining this, tracking it, and keeping an eye out for violations is an incredible waste of time—time that could be spent actually writing code. It's for this very reason that we advocate tracking credit at the *project level*, not in the code itself. Most projects that we've seen have an "Authors" or "Contributors" file that lists everyone who has done work. If you need more detail, your version control system can tell you. Of course, if you *don't* use version control, all those moments will be lost in time, like tears in rain.[17]

REQUIRE CODE REVIEWS FOR EVERY COMMIT

If you're going to have coding standards, you need to have a means of monitoring code going into your product. Whether you review the code before committing it or after committing it, you should make sure every line of code that goes into your repository gets a second pair of eyes on it to check for style, quality, and, of course, careless mistakes. Keep code changes small and reviewable—changesets that are thousands of lines long are unreviewable for anything but formatting nits. This not only results in a higher-quality code base, but also goes a long way toward instilling a strong sense of group pride in the quality of your code. For more information, see the section on feedback loops in "Hiding Is Considered Harmful" on page 5.

HAVE REAL TEST AND RELEASE PROCESSES

Whether you're a full-on test-driven development shop or you just have some simple regression tests for your product, the more automated tests you have for your product, the more confident you can be when you're tearing through fixing bugs or adding new features. Once your team determines the role that testing will play, it should be part of the coding and review process. Just as importantly, your release process should be lightweight enough that you can do frequent

---

17 Roy, *Blade Runner*, 1982.

releases (e.g., weekly), but thorough enough that you catch brokenness before it hits your users.

It Really Is About Your Product, After All

Although these habits of culture and communication may seem to represent a certain amount of bias, as they reflect the manner in which we prefer to work, it's not as subjective as you might think. We've found that building a strong, productive team culture and taking some time to pay attention to communication in the team creates a team that will spend more time writing and shipping product and less time arguing about what product to ship.

Strong teams don't arise spontaneously; they're carefully seeded and cultivated by team leads and founders who understand the high cost of trying to write software with a dysfunctional team. Putting this work in from the outset helps to create a self-selecting culture that builds a team that will spend much more time designing and creating a product than defining and defending their culture. A big side benefit of this effort—communication and process—is that it drastically reduces the barrier to entry for newcomers to your team. Without these elements in place, newcomers will either waste a lot of time struggling to learn how your team works or give up and try to make your team work like their last team did (for good or for bad).

While getting the right people on your team and the right values instilled in your team is important, the overwhelming majority of effort that goes into a culture turns out to be communication. Mission statements, meetings, mailing lists, online chat, code comments, documentation, and even decision-making processes all make up the many different ways your team communicates, both with itself and with others. It's often a surprise to people that it takes so much communication—including emotional time and effort—to build a strong team for the sole purpose of creating a product, but it's true. Your product is ultimately about communications with *people*, not just with a machine.

No matter what your team's culture is, and regardless of how well your team communicates, every effective team that we've ever seen has a leader. In the next chapter, we'll look into what makes the most effective team leader, why her role is probably not what you think, and why it's important for every team member to understand the basics of leading a team.

of a product, while a TLM is responsible for the technical direction for all (or part) of a product in addition to the careers and happiness of the people on the team. This enables those who want to focus on leading a project to avoid the people management part of being a leader if they want to.

THE ONLY THING TO FEAR IS...WELL, EVERYTHING

Aside from the general sense of malaise that most people feel when they hear the word *manager*, there are a number of reasons that most people don't want to become managers. The biggest reason you'll hear in the software development world is that you spend much less time writing code, which is true whether you're a technical leader or a people leader. We'll talk more about that later, but first, some more reasons why most of us avoid becoming managers.

If you've spent the majority of your career writing code, you typically end a day with something you can point to—whether it's code, a design document, or a pile of bugs you just closed—and say, "That's what I did today." Based on this metric of productivity, at the end of a busy day of "management" you'll usually find yourself thinking, "I didn't do a *damned thing* today." It's the equivalent of spending years counting the number of apples you picked each day, and changing to a job picking bananas, only to say to yourself at the end of each day, "I didn't pick any apples," handily ignoring the giant pile of bananas sitting next to you. Quantifying management work *is* more difficult than counting widgets you turned out, and you don't have to take credit for your team's work; however, making it possible for them to be happy and productive is a big measure of your job. Just don't fall into the trap of counting apples when you're picking bananas.

Another big reason for not becoming a manager is often unspoken but rooted in the famous "Peter Principle," which states that, "In a hierarchy every employee tends to rise to his level of incompetence." Most people have had a manager who was incapable of doing her job or was just really bad at managing people,[7] and we know some people who have *only* worked for bad managers. If you've only been exposed to crappy managers for your entire career, why would you ever want to *be* a manager? Why would you want to be promoted to a role that you weren't able to do?

There are great reasons to consider becoming a manager: first, it's a way to scale yourself. Even if you're great at writing code, there's still an upper limit to the amount of code you can write. Imagine how much code a team of great engineers could write under your leadership! Second, you might just be really good at it—many people who find themselves sucked into the leadership vacuum of a project discover that they're exceptionally skilled at providing the kind of guidance, help, and air cover a team needs.

The Servant Leader

There seems to be a sort of disease that strikes new managers where they forget about all the awful things *their* managers did to them and suddenly start doing these same things to "manage" the people that report to them. The symptoms of this disease include, but are by no means limited to, micromanaging, ignoring low performers, and hiring pushovers. Without prompt treatment, this disease can kill an entire team. The best advice we got when we first became managers at Google was from Steve Vinter, an engineering director. He said, "Above all, resist the urge to manage." One of the greatest urges of the newly minted manager is to actively "manage" her employees because that's what a manager does, right? This typically has disastrous consequences.

The cure for the "management" disease is a liberal application of what we call "servant leadership," which is a nice way of saying the most important thing a leader can do is to serve her team, much like a butler or majordomo tends to the health and well-being of a household. As a servant leader, you should strive to create an atmosphere of humility, respect, and trust (HRT). This may mean

---

7 Yet another reason companies shouldn't force people into management as part of a career path: if an engineer is able to write reams of great code and has no desire at all to manage people or lead a team, by forcing her into a management or tech lead role you're losing a great engineer and gaining a crappy manager. This is not only a bad idea, but it's actively harmful.

removing bureaucratic obstacles that a team member can't remove by herself, helping a team achieve consensus, or even buying dinner for the team when they're working late at the office. The servant leader fills in the cracks to smooth the way for her team and advises them when necessary, but still isn't afraid of getting her hands dirty. The only managing that a servant leader does is to manage both the technical *and* social health of the team; as tempting as it may be to focus purely on the technical health of the team, the social health of the team is just as important (but often infinitely harder to manage!).

Antipatterns

Before we go over a litany of "design patterns" for successful leaders, we're going to review a collection of the patterns you *don't* want to follow if you want to be a successful leader. We've observed these destructive patterns in a handful of bad leaders we've encountered in our careers, and in more than a few cases, ourselves.[8]

ANTIPATTERN: HIRE PUSHOVERS

If you're a manager and you're feeling insecure in your role (for whatever reason), one way to make sure no one questions your authority or threatens your job is to hire people you can push around. You can achieve this by hiring people who aren't as smart or ambitious as you are, or just people who are more insecure than you. While this will cement your position as the team leader and decision maker, it will mean a lot more work for you. Your team won't be able to make a move without you leading them like dogs on a leash. If you build a team of pushovers, you probably can't take a vacation; the moment you leave the room, productivity comes to a screeching halt. But surely this is a small price to pay for feeling secure in your job, right?

Instead, you should strive to hire people who are smarter than you and can replace you. This can be difficult because these very same people will challenge you on a regular basis (in addition to letting you know in no uncertain terms when you screw up). These very same people will also consistently impress you and make great things happen. They'll be able to direct themselves to a much greater extent, and some will be eager to lead the team as well. You shouldn't see this as an attempt to usurp your power, but rather as an opportunity for you to lead an additional team, investigate new opportunities, or even take a vacation

---

8 See the section on failure, in Chapter 2.

without worrying about checking in on the team every day to make sure they're getting their work done.

ANTIPATTERN: IGNORE LOW PERFORMERS

Early in Fitz's career as a team leader at Google, the time came for him to hand out bonus letters to his team, and he grinned as he told his manager, "I *love* being a manager!" Without missing a beat, Fitz's manager, a long-time industry veteran, replied, "Sometimes you get to be the tooth fairy, other times you have to be the dentist."

It's never any fun to pull teeth. We've seen team leaders do all the right things to build incredibly strong teams, only to have these teams fail to excel (and eventually fall apart) because of just one or two low performers. We understand that the human aspect is the hardest part of writing software, but the hardest part of dealing with humans is handling someone who isn't meeting expectations. Sometimes people miss expectations because they're not working long enough or hard enough, but the most difficult cases are when someone just isn't capable of doing his job no matter how long or hard he works.

The team at Google that is responsible for keeping all of their services running has a motto: "Hope is not a strategy." And nowhere is hope more overused as a strategy than in dealing with a low performer. Most team leaders grit their teeth, avert their eyes, and just hope that the low performer either magically gets better or just goes away. Yet it is extremely rare that this person does either.

While the leader is hoping and the low performer isn't getting better (or leaving), high performers on the team waste valuable time pulling the low performer along and team morale leaks away into the ether. You can be sure that the team knows they're there even if you're ignoring them—the rest of the team is acutely aware of who the low performers are, because they have to carry them.

Ignoring low performers is also a way to keep new high performers from joining your team, and a way to encourage existing high performers to leave. You eventually wind up with a whole team of low performers because they're the only ones who *can't* leave of their own volition. Lastly, you aren't even doing *the low performer* any favors by keeping him on the team; often, someone who wouldn't do well on your team would actually have plenty of impact somewhere else.

The benefit of dealing with a low performer as quickly as possible is that you can put yourself in the position of helping him up *or* out. If you deal with a low performer right away, you'll oftentimes find that he merely needs some encouragement or direction to slip into a higher state of productivity. If you wait too long to deal with a low performer, his relationship with the team is going to be so sour and you're going to be so frustrated that you're not going to be able to help him.

How does one coach a low performer effectively? It turns out that the two of us have (unfortunately) had quite a lot of experience in this area, gained through painful trial and error. The best analogy is to imagine you're helping a limping person learn to walk again, then jog, then run alongside the rest of the team. It almost always requires temporary micromanagement—but still a whole lot of HRT, particularly respect. Set up a specific time frame (say, two or three months), and some very specific goals you expect him to achieve in that period. Make the goals small and incremental, so there's an opportunity for lots of small successes. Meet with the team member every week to check on progress, and be sure you set really explicit expectations around each upcoming milestone, so it's easy to measure success or failure. If the low performer can't keep up, it will become quite obvious to *both* of you early in the process. At this point, the person will often acknowledge that things aren't going well and decide to quit; in other cases, determination will kick in and he'll "up his game" to meet expectations. Either way, by working directly with the low performer you're catalyzing important and necessary changes.

ANTIPATTERN: IGNORE HUMAN ISSUES

As we've said before, a team leader has two major areas of focus for his team: the social and the technical. It's rather common for leaders to be stronger in the technical side, and since most leaders are promoted from a technical job (where the primary goal of their job was to solve technical problems), they tend to ignore human issues. It's tempting to focus all your energy on the technical side of your team because, as an individual contributor, you spend the vast majority of your time solving technical problems. When you were a student, your classes were all about learning the technical ins and outs of your work. Now that you're a leader, however, you ignore the human element of your team at your own peril.

Let's start with an example of a leader ignoring the human element in his team. Years ago, a close friend of Fitz's—we'll call him Jake—had his first child. Jake and Fitz had worked together for years, both remotely and in the same office, so in the weeks following the arrival of the new baby, Jake worked from home. This worked out great for Jake and his wife, and Fitz was totally fine with it as he was already used to working remotely with Jake. They were their usual productive selves until their manager, Pablo (who worked in a different office), found out that Jake was working from home for most of the week. Pablo was upset that Jake wasn't going into the office to work with Fitz, despite the fact that

Jake was just as productive as always and that Fitz was fine with the situation. Jake attempted to explain to Pablo that he was just as productive as he would be if he came into the office, and that it was much easier on both him and his wife for him to mostly work from home for a few weeks. Pablo's response: "Dude, people have kids *all the time*. You need to go into the office." Needless to say, Jake (normally a mild-mannered engineer) was enraged and lost a lot of respect for Pablo.

There are numerous ways that Pablo could have handled this differently: he could have showed some understanding that Jake wanted to be home more for his wife and, if his productivity and team weren't being affected, just let him continue to do so for a while. He could have negotiated that Jake go into the office for one or two days a week until things settled down. Regardless of the end result, a little bit of empathy would have gone a long way toward keeping Jake happy in this situation.

ANTIPATTERN: BE EVERYONE'S FRIEND

The first foray that most people have into leadership is when they become the lead of a team of which they were formerly members. Many leads don't want to lose the friendships they've cultivated with their teams, so they will sometimes work extra hard to maintain friendships with their team members after becoming a team lead. This can be a recipe for disaster and for a lot of broken friendships. Don't confuse friendship with leading with a soft touch: when you hold power over someone's career, he may feel pressure to artificially reciprocate gestures of friendship.

Remember that you can lead a team and build consensus without being a peer of your team (or a monumental hard-ass). Likewise, you can be a tough leader without tossing your existing friendships to the wind. We've found that having lunch with your team can be an effective way to stay socially connected to them without making them uncomfortable—this gives you a chance to have informal conversations outside the normal work environment.

Sometimes it can be tricky to move into a management role over someone who has been a good friend and a peer. If the friend who is being managed is not self-managing and is not a hard worker, it can be stressful for everyone. We recommend that you avoid getting into this situation whenever possible.

ANTIPATTERN: COMPROMISE THE HIRING BAR

Steve Jobs once said: "*A people hire other A people; B people hire C people.*" It's incredibly easy to fall victim to this adage, and even more so when you're trying to hire quickly. A common approach we've seen is that a team needs to hire five engineers, so they sift through their pile of applications, interview 40 or 50 people, and pick the best 5 *regardless of whether they meet the hiring bar.* This is one of the fastest ways to build a mediocre team.

The cost of finding the right person—whether by paying recruiters, paying advertising, or pounding the pavement for references—pales in comparison to the cost of dealing with an employee you never should have hired in the first place. This "cost" manifests itself in lost team productivity, team stress, time spent managing the employee up or out, and the paperwork and stress involved in firing the employee. That's assuming, of course, that you try to avoid the monumental cost of just leaving him on the team. If you're managing a team where you don't have a say over hiring and you're unhappy with the hires being made for your team, you need to fight tooth and nail for higher-quality engineers. If you still keep getting handed substandard engineers, maybe it's time to look for another job. Without the raw materials for a great team, you're doomed.

ANTIPATTERN: TREAT YOUR TEAM LIKE CHILDREN

The best way to show your team you don't trust them is to treat them like kids—people tend to act the way you treat them, so if you treat them like children or prisoners, don't be surprised when that's how they behave. You can manifest this behavior by micromanaging them or simply by being disrespectful of their abilities and giving them no opportunity to be responsible for their work. If it's permanently necessary to micromanage people because you don't trust them, you've got a hiring failure on your hands. Well, it's a failure unless your goal was to build a team that you can spend the rest of your life babysitting. If you hire people worthy of trust and show these people you trust them, they'll usually rise to the occasion (sticking with the basic premise, as we mentioned earlier, that you've hired good people).

Fitz runs a conference in Chicago that used to be at a site rented from a local institution. The first time Fitz went to get access to the venue for the conference, the facilities manager gave Fitz a brief tour of the place to make sure he knew where everything was. The manager then handed him the key to the building and told Fitz that he'd get the key back from him next week. There was no list of "dos and dont's," and no extensive supervision for the event, and as a result Fitz and his team felt responsible for taking take care of the facility as though it were their own, going above and beyond the expectations of keeping the place clean and organized.

The results of this level of trust go all the way from keys to a building to office and computer supplies. As another example, Google provides employees with cabinets stocked with various and sundry office supplies (e.g., pens, notebooks, and other "legacy" implements of creation) that are free to take as employees need them. The IT department runs numerous "Tech Stops" that provide self-service areas that are like a mini electronics store. These contain lots of computer accessories and doodads (e.g., power supplies, cables, mice, USB drives, etc.) that would be easy to just grab and walk off with, but since Google employees are being entrusted to check these items out, they feel a responsibility to Do The Right Thing. Many people from typical corporations react in horror to hearing this, exclaiming that surely Google is hemorrhaging money due to people "stealing" these items. That's certainly possible, but what about the costs of having a workforce that behaves like children? Surely that's more expensive than the price of a few pens and USB cables.

Leadership Patterns

These are a collection of behavior patterns for successful leadership that we've learned from experience, from watching other successful leaders, and, most of all, from our own leadership mentors. These patterns are not only those that we've had great success implementing, but the patterns that we've always respected the most in the leaders that we follow.

LOSE THE EGO

We talked about "losing the ego" in Chapter 1 when we first examined HRT, but it's especially important when you're playing the role of servant leader. This pattern is frequently misunderstood as encouraging leaders to be a doormat and let their team walk all over them, but that's not the case at all. We admit that there's a fine line between being humble and letting others take advantage of you, but humility is *not* the same as lacking confidence. You can still have self-confidence and opinions without being an egomaniac. Big personal egos are hard to handle on any team, especially in the team's leader. Instead, you should work to cultivate a strong collective *team* ego and identity.

Part of "losing the ego" is something we've covered already: you need to trust your team. That means respecting the abilities and prior accomplishments of the team members, even if they're new to your team.

If you're not micromanaging your team, you can be pretty certain the folks working in the trenches know the details of their work better than you do. This means that while you may be the one driving the team to consensus and helping to set the direction, the nuts and bolts of how to accomplish your goals are best decided by the people who are putting the product together. This gives them not only a greater sense of ownership, but also a greater sense of accountability and responsibility for the success (or failure!) of their product. If you've got a good team and you let them set the bar for the quality and rate of their work, they'll accomplish more than they would by you standing over them with a carrot and a stick.

Most people new to a leadership role feel an enormous responsibility to get everything right, to know everything, and to have all the answers. We can assure you that you will not get everything right, nor will you have all the answers, and if you act like you do, you'll quickly lose the respect of your team. A lot of this comes down to having a basic sense of security in your role. Think back to when you were an individual contributor; you could smell insecurity a mile away. Try to appreciate inquiry: when someone questions a decision or statement you made, remember that this person is usually just trying to better understand you. If you encourage inquiry, you're much more likely to get the kind of constructive criticism that will make you a better leader of a better team. Finding people who will give you good constructive criticism is incredibly difficult, and it's even harder to get this kind of criticism from people who "work for you." Think about the big picture of what you're trying to accomplish as a team, and accept feedback and criticism openly; avoid the urge to be territorial.

The last part of losing the ego is a simple one, but many engineers would rather be boiled in oil than do it: apologize when you make a mistake. And we don't mean you should just sprinkle "I'm sorry" throughout your conversation like salt on popcorn—you have to sincerely mean it. You are absolutely going to make mistakes, and whether you admit it or not your team is going to know you've made a mistake. They'll know regardless of whether they talk to you or not (and one thing is guaranteed: they *will* talk about it with one another). Apologizing doesn't cost money. People have enormous respect for leaders who apologize when they screw up, and contrary to popular belief it doesn't make you vulnerable. In fact, you'll usually gain respect from people when you apologize, because apologizing tells people you are level-headed, good at assessing situations, and—coming back to HRT—humble.

BE A ZEN MASTER

As an engineer, you likely developed an excellent sense of skepticism and cynicism, but this can be a liability when you're trying to lead a team. That's not to say you should be naïvely optimistic at every turn, but you would do well to be less vocally skeptical while still letting your team know you're aware of the intricacies and obstacles involved in your work. Mediating your reactions and maintaining your calm is more important as you lead more people, because your team will (both unconsciously and consciously) look to you for clues on how to act and react to whatever is going on around you.

A simple way to visualize this effect is to see your company's org chart as a chain of gears, with the individual contributor as a tiny gear with just a few teeth all the way at one end, and each successive manager above her as another gear, ending with the CEO as the largest gear with many hundreds of teeth. This means every time that individual's "manager gear" (with maybe a few dozen teeth) makes a single revolution, the "individual's gear" makes two or three revolutions. And the CEO can make a small movement and send the hapless employee, at the end of a chain of six or seven gears, spinning wildly! The farther you move up the chain, the faster you can set the gears below you spinning, whether you intend to or not.

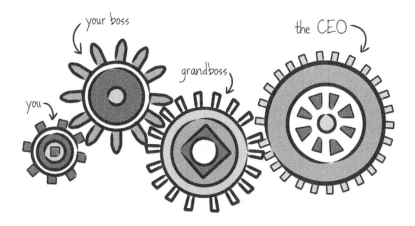

Another way of thinking about this is the maxim that the *leader is always on stage*. This means that if you're in an overt leadership position, you are always being watched: not just when you run a meeting or give a talk, but even when you're just sitting at your desk answering emails. Your peers are watching you for subtle clues in your body language, your reactions to small talk, and your signals as you eat lunch. Do they read confidence or fear? As a leader, your job is to inspire, but inspiration is a 24/7 job. Your visible attitude about absolutely everything—no matter how trivial—is unconsciously noticed and spreads infectiously to your team.

Fitz had a manager, Bill,[9] who truly mastered the ability to maintain calm at all times. No matter what blew up, no matter what crazy thing happened, no matter how big the firestorm, Bill would never panic. Most of the time he'd place one arm across his chest, rest his chin in his hand, and ask questions about the problem, usually to a completely panicked employee. This had the effect of calming her and helping her to focus on solving the problem instead of running around in a chicken-with-its-head-cut-off mode. Fitz used to joke that if someone came in and told Bill 19 of the company's offices had been attacked by space aliens, Bill's response would be, "Any idea why they didn't make it an even 20?"

---

9 His real name.

This brings us to another Zen management trick: asking questions. When a team member asks you for advice, it's usually pretty exciting because you're finally getting the chance to fix something! That's exactly what you did for years before moving into a leadership position, so you usually go *leaping* into solution mode, but that is the last place you should be. The person asking for advice typically doesn't want you to solve her problem, but rather to help *her* solve it, and the easiest way to do this is to ask her questions. This isn't to say you should replace yourself with a Magic 8 Ball, which would be maddening and unhelpful. Instead, you can apply some HRT and try to help her solve the problem on her own by trying to refine and explore her problem. This will usually lead the employee to the answer,[10] and it will be *her* answer, which leads back to the ownership and responsibility we went over earlier in this chapter. Whether you have the answer or not, using this technique will almost always leave the employee with the impression that you did. Tricky, eh? Socrates would be proud of you.

BE A CATALYST

In chemistry a catalyst is something that accelerates a chemical reaction, but which itself is not consumed in the reaction. One of the ways in which catalysts (e.g., enzymes) work is to bring reactants into close proximity: instead of bouncing around randomly in a solution, the reactants are much more likely to favorably interact with one another when the catalyst helps bring them together. This is a role you'll often need to play as a leader, and there are a number of ways you can go about it.

One of the most common things a team leader does is to build consensus. This may mean you drive the process from start to finish, or you just give it a gentle push in the right direction to speed it up. Working to build team consensus is a leadership skill that is often used by unofficial leaders because it's one way you can lead without any actual authority. If you have the authority, you can direct and dictate direction, but that's less effective overall than building consensus. If your team is looking to move quickly, sometimes they'll voluntarily concede authority and direction to one or more team leads. While this might look like a dictatorship or oligarchy, when it's done voluntarily it's a form of consensus.

---

10 See also "Rubber duck debugging," *http://en.wikipedia.org/wiki/Rubber_duck_debugging.*

Know Where to Put the Chalk Mark

There's a story about a Master of all things mechanical who had long since retired. His former company was having a problem that no one could fix, so they called in the Master to see if he could help find the problem. The Master examined the machine, listened to it, and eventually pulled out a worn piece of chalk and made a small X on the side of the machine. He informed the technician that there was a loose wire that needed repair at that very spot. The technician opened the machine and tightened the loose wire, thus fixing the problem. When the Master's invoice arrived for $10,000, the irate CEO wrote back demanding a breakdown for this ridiculously high charge for a simple chalk mark! The Master responded with another invoice, showing a $1 cost for the chalk to make the mark, and $9,999 for knowing where to put it.

To us, this is a story about wisdom: that a single, carefully considered adjustment can have gigantic effects. Ben tries to use this technique when managing people. He imagines his team as flying around in a great blimp, headed slowly and surely in a certain direction. Instead of micromanaging and trying to make continuous course corrections, he spends most of his week carefully watching and listening. At the end of the week he makes a small chalk mark in a precise location on the blimp, then gives a small but critical "tap" to adjust the course.

Sometimes your team already has consensus about what you need to do, but they hit a roadblock and get stuck. This could be a technical or organizational roadblock, but jumping in to help the team get moving again is a common leadership technique. There are some roadblocks that, while virtually impossible for your team members to get past, will be easy for you to handle, and helping your team to understand that you're glad (and able) to help out with these roadblocks is valuable.

One time Fitz's team spent several weeks trying to work past an obstacle with his company's legal department. When they finally reached their wits' end and came to Fitz with the problem, he had it solved in less than two hours because he knew the right person to contact. Another time Ben's team needed some server resources and just couldn't get them allocated. Fortunately, Ben was in communication with other teams across the company and managed to get the team exactly what they needed that very afternoon. Yet another time one of the engineers on Fitz's team was having trouble with an arcane bit of Java code, and while Fitz wasn't a Java expert, he was able to connect the engineer to another engineer who knew exactly what the problem was. You don't have to know all the answers to help remove roadblocks, but it usually helps to know the people who do. *In many cases, knowing the right person is more valuable than knowing the right answer.*

FAILURE IS AN OPTION

Another way to catalyze your team is to make them feel safe and secure so that they can take greater risks. Risk is a fascinating thing—most humans are *terrible* at evaluating risk, and most companies try to avoid risk at all costs. As a result of this, the usual modus operandi is to work conservatively and focus on smaller successes even when taking a bigger risk might mean exponentially greater success. A common saying at Google is that if you try to achieve an impossible goal, there's a good chance you'll fail, but if you fail trying to achieve the impossible, you'll most likely accomplish way more than you would have accomplished had you merely attempted something you knew you could complete. A good way to build a culture where risk taking is accepted is to let your team *know* it's OK to fail.

So let's get that out of the way: it's OK to fail. In fact, we like to think of failure as a way of learning a lot really quickly (providing that you're not repeatedly failing at the same thing). In addition, it's important to see failure as an opportunity to learn and not to point fingers or assign blame. Failing fast is good, because there's not a lot at stake.[11] Failing slowly can also teach a valuable lesson, but it is more painful because more is at risk and more can be lost (usually engineering time). Failing in a manner that affects your customers is probably the least desirable failure that we encounter, and one where we have the greatest amount of structure in place to learn from failures. As mentioned earlier, every time there is a production failure at Google, they perform a postmortem. This procedure is a way to document the events that led to the actual failure and to develop a series of steps that will prevent it from happening in the future. This is not an opportunity to point fingers, nor is it intended to introduce unnecessary bureaucratic checks; the goal is rather to focus strongly on the core of the problem and fix it once and for all. It's very difficult, but quite effective (and cathartic!).

---

11 See Alberto Savoia's talk, "The Pretotyping Manifesto" (*http://bit.ly/pretotyping_manifesto*).

Individual successes and failures are a bit different. It's one thing to laud individual successes, but looking to assign individual blame in the case of failure is a great way to divide a team and discourage risk taking across the board. It's OK to fail, but fail as a team and learn from your failures. If an individual succeeds, praise him in front of the team. If an individual fails, give constructive criticism in private.[12] Whatever the case, take advantage of the opportunity and apply a liberal helping of HRT to help your team to learn from their failures.

BE A TEACHER AND A MENTOR

One of the hardest things to do as a team leader is to watch a more junior-level team member spend three hours working on something you *know* you can knock out in 20 minutes. Teaching people and giving them a chance to learn on their own can be incredibly difficult at first, but it's a vital component of effective leadership. This is especially important for new hires who, in addition to learning your team's technology and code base, are learning your team's culture and the appropriate level of responsibility to assume.

Much like the role of manager, most people don't apply for the role of mentor—they usually become one when a team lead is looking for someone to mentor a new team member. It doesn't take a lot of formal education or preparation to be a mentor; in fact, you primarily need three things: experience with your team's processes and systems, the ability to explain things to someone else, and the ability to gauge how much help your mentee needs. The last thing is probably the most important—giving your mentee enough information is what you're supposed to be doing, but if you overexplain things or ramble on endlessly, your mentee will probably tune you out rather than politely tell you she got it.

SET CLEAR GOALS

This is one of those patterns that, as obvious as it sounds, is solidly ignored by an enormous number of leaders. If you're going to get your team moving rapidly in one direction, you need to make sure they all understand and agree on what the direction is. Imagine your product is a big truck (and not a series of tubes). Each team member has in his hand a rope tied to the front of the truck, and as he works on the product, he'll pull the truck in his own direction. If your intention is to pull the truck (or product) northbound as quickly as possible, you can't have

---

12 Public criticism of an individual is rarely necessary, and most often is just mean or cruel. You can be sure the rest of the team already knows when an individual has failed, so there's no need to rub it in.

team members pulling every which way—you want them all pulling the truck north.

The easiest way to set a clear goal and get your team pulling the product in the same direction is to create a concise mission statement for the team (see the section "The Mission Statement—No, Really" on page 33 in Chapter 2 for more information about mission statements). Once you've helped the team define their direction and goals, you can step back and give them more autonomy, periodically checking in to make sure they're still on the right track. This not only frees up your time to handle other leadership tasks, but it also *drastically increases the efficiency of your team*. Teams can (and do) succeed without clear goals, but they typically waste a great deal of energy as each team member pulls the product in a slightly different direction. This frustrates you, slows progress for the team, and forces you to use more and more of your own energy to correct the course.

BE HONEST

This doesn't mean we're assuming you are lying to your team, but it merits a mention because you'll inevitably find yourself in a position where you can't tell your team something or, even worse, you have to tell them something they don't want to hear. A former manager of Fitz's would tell new team members, "I won't lie to you, but I will tell you when I can't tell you something or if I just don't know."

If a team member approaches you about something you can't share with her, it's OK to just tell her you know the answer but can't tell her. Even more common is when a team member asks you something you don't know the answer to: you can tell her you don't know. This is another one of those things that seems blindingly obvious when you read it, but many people move to a manager role and feel that if they don't know the answer to something it proves they're weak or out of touch. In reality, the only thing it proves is that they're human.

Giving hard feedback is...well, *hard*. The first time you have to tell one of your reports that he made a mistake or didn't do his job as well as was expected of him can be incredibly stressful. Most management texts advise that you use the "compliment sandwich" to soften the blow when delivering hard feedback. A compliment sandwich looks something like this:

"You're a solid member of the team and one of our smartest engineers. That being said, your code is incredibly convoluted and almost impossible for anyone else on the team to understand. But you've got great potential and a wicked cool neckbeard."

Sure, this softens the blow, but with this sort of beating around the bush most people will walk out of this meeting only thinking, "Sweet! I've got a wicked cool beard!" We *strongly* advise against using the compliment sandwich, not because we think you should be unnecessarily cruel or harsh, but *because most people won't hear the critical message*, which is that something needs to change. It's possible to employ HRT here: be kind and empathetic when delivering constructive criticism without resorting to the compliment sandwich. In fact, kindness and empathy are *critical* if you want the recipient to hear the criticism and not immediately go on the defensive.

Years ago, Fitz picked up a team member, Tim, from another manager who insisted that Tim was impossible to work with. He told Fitz that Tim never responded to feedback or criticism and instead just kept doing the same things he'd been told he shouldn't do. Fitz sat in on a few of the manager's meetings with Tim to watch the interaction between the manager and Tim, and he noticed that the manager made extensive use of the compliment sandwich so as not to hurt Tim's feelings. When Fitz took Tim on his team, he sat down with him and very clearly explained that Tim needed to make some changes to work more effectively with the team. Fitz didn't give Tim any compliments or candy-coat the issue, but just as importantly, Fitz wasn't mean—he just laid out the facts as he saw them based on Tim's performance with the previous team. Lo and behold, within a matter of weeks (and after a few more "refresher" meetings), Tim's performance improved dramatically. Tim just needed very clear feedback and direction.

When you're providing direct feedback or criticism, your delivery is key to making sure your message is heard and not deflected. If you put the recipient on the defensive, he's not going to be thinking of how he can change, but rather how he can argue with you to show you you're wrong. Ben once managed an engineer we'll call Dean. Dean had extremely strong opinions and would argue with the rest of the team about *anything*. It could be something as big as the team's mission or as small as the placement of a widget on a web page; Dean would argue with the same conviction and vehemence either way, and he refused to let anything slide. After months of this behavior, Ben met with Dean to explain to him that he was being too combative. Now, if Ben had just said, "Dean, stop being such a jerk," you can be pretty sure Dean would have disregarded it entirely. Ben thought hard about how he could get Dean to understand how his actions were adversely affecting the team, and he came up with the following metaphor:

> Every time a decision is made, it's like a train coming through town—when you jump in front of the train to stop it you slow the train down and potentially annoy the engineer driving the train. A new train comes by every 15 minutes, and if you jump in front of every train, not only do you spend a lot of your time stopping trains, but eventually one of the engineers driving the train is going to get mad enough to run right over you. So, while it's OK to jump in front of some trains, pick and choose the ones you want to stop to make sure you're only stopping the trains that really matter.

This anecdote not only injected a bit of humor into the situation, but also made it easier for Ben and Dean to discuss the effect that Dean's "train stopping" was having on the team in addition to the energy Dean was spending on it.

TRACK HAPPINESS

As a leader, one way you can make your team more productive (and less likely to leave) in the long term is to take some time to gauge their happiness. The best leaders we've worked with have all been amateur psychologists, looking in on their team members' welfare from time to time, making sure they get recognition for what they do, and trying to make certain they are happy with their work. One leader we know makes a spreadsheet of all the grungy, thankless tasks that need to be done and makes certain these tasks are evenly spread across the team. Another leader watches the hours his team is working and uses comp time and fun team outings to avoid burnout and exhaustion. Yet another leader starts one-on-one sessions with his team members by dealing with their technical issues as a way to break the ice, and then takes some time to make sure each engineer has everything he needs to get his work done. After they've warmed up, he talks to the engineer for a bit about how he's enjoying the work he's doing and what he's looking forward to next.

One of the most valuable tools in tracking your team's happiness is, at the end of each one-on-one meeting, to ask the team member, "What do you need?" This simple question is a great way to wrap up and make sure each team member has what he needs to be productive and happy, although you may need to carefully probe a bit to get details. If you ask this every time you have a one-on-one, you'll find that eventually your team will remember this and sometimes even come to you with a laundry list of things they need to make their job better.

The Unexpected Question

Shortly after Fitz started at Google he had his first meeting with then-CEO Eric Schmidt, and at the end Eric asked Fitz, "Is there anything you need?" Fitz, who had prepared a million defensive responses to hard questions or challenges, was *completely* unprepared for this. So he sat there dumbstruck and staring. But you can be sure Fitz had something ready the next time he was asked that question!

It can also be worthwhile to pay some attention to your team's happiness *outside* the office. Be wary of assuming that people have no life outside of work—having unrealistic expectations about the amount of time people can put into their work will cause people to lose respect for you, or worse, to burn out. We're not advocating that you pry into your team members' personal lives, but being sensitive to personal situations that your team members are going through can give you a lot of insight into why they may be more or less productive at any given time. Giving a little extra slack to a team member who is having a tough time at home now can make him a lot more willing to put in longer hours when your team has a tight deadline to hit later.

A big part of tracking your team members' happiness is tracking their careers. If you ask a team member where she sees her career in five years, most of the time you'll get a shrug and a blank look. When put on the spot, most people won't say much about this, but there are usually a few things that everyone would like to do in the next five years: get promoted, learn something new, launch something important, and work with smart people. Regardless of whether they verbalize this, most people are thinking about it. If you're going to be an effective leader, you should be thinking about how you can help make all those things happen and let your team know you're thinking about this. The most important part of this is to take these implicit goals and make them *explicit* so that when you're giving career advice you have a real set of metrics on which to evaluate situations and opportunities.

Tracking happiness comes down to not just monitoring careers, but also giving your team members opportunities to improve themselves, get recognized for the work they do, and have a little fun along the way.

OTHER TIPS AND TRICKS

Delegate, but get your hands dirty. When moving from an individual contributor role to a leadership role, achieving a balance is one of the hardest things to do: initially, you're inclined to do all of the work yourself, and after being in a leadership role for a long time, it's easy to get into the habit of doing *none* of the work yourself. If you're new to a leadership role, you probably need to work hard to delegate work to other engineers on your team, even if it will take them a lot longer than you to accomplish that work. Not only is this one way for you to maintain your sanity, but also it's how the rest of your team will learn. If you've been leading teams for a while or if you pick up a new team, one of the easiest ways to gain the team's respect and get up to speed on what they're doing is to get your hands dirty—usually by taking on a grungy task no one else wants to do. You can have a résumé and a list of achievements a mile long, but nothing lets a team know how skillful and dedicated (and humble) you are like jumping in and actually doing some hard work.

Seek to replace yourself. Unless you want to keep doing the exact same job for the rest of your career, seek to replace yourself. This starts, as we mentioned earlier, with the hiring process: if you want a member of your team to replace you, you need to hire people capable of replacing you, which we usually sum up by saying you need to "hire people smarter than you." Once you have team members capable of doing your job, you need to give them opportunities to take on more responsibilities or occasionally lead the team. If you do this, you'll quickly see who has the most aptitude to lead as well as who *wants* to lead the team. Remember that some people prefer to just be high-performing individual contributors, and that's OK. We've always been amazed at companies that take their best engineers and—against their wishes—throw these engineers into management roles. This usually subtracts a great engineer from your team and adds a subpar manager.

Know when to make waves. You will (inevitably and frequently) have difficult situations crop up where every cell in your body is screaming at you to do nothing about it. It may be the engineer on your team whose technical chops aren't up to par. It may be the person who jumps in front of every train. It may be the unmotivated employee who is working 30 hours a week. "Just wait a bit and it will get better," you'll tell yourself. "It will work itself out," you'll rationalize. Don't fall into this trap—these are the situations where you *need* to make the biggest waves and you need to make them now. Rarely will these problems work themselves out, and the longer you wait to address them, the more they'll adversely affect the rest of the team and the more they'll keep you up at night thinking about them. By waiting, you're only delaying the inevitable and causing untold damage in the process. So act, and act quickly.

Shield your team from chaos. When you step into a leadership role, the first thing you'll usually discover is that outside your team is a world of chaos and uncertainty (or even insanity) that you never saw when you were an individual contributor. When Fitz first became a manager back in the 1990s (before going back to being an individual contributor) he was taken aback by the sheer volume of uncertainty and organizational chaos that was happening in his company. He asked another manager what had caused this sudden rockiness in the otherwise calm company, and the other manager laughed hysterically at Fitz's naïveté: the chaos had always been present, but Fitz's previous manager had shielded Fitz and the rest of the team from it.

Give your team air cover. While it's important that you keep your team informed about what's going on "above" them in the company, it's just as important that you defend them from a lot of the uncertainty and frivolous demands that may be imposed upon you from outside your team. Share as much information as you can with your team, but don't distract them with organizational craziness that is extremely unlikely to ever actually affect them.

Let your team know when they're doing well. Many new team leads can get so caught up in dealing with the shortcomings of their team members that they neglect to provide positive feedback often enough. Just as you let someone know when he screws up, be sure to let him know when he does well, and be sure to let him (and the rest of the team) know when he knocks one out of the park.

Lastly, here's something the best leaders know and use often when they have adventurous team members who want to try new things often: it's easy to say "yes" if it's easy to undo something. If you have a team member who wants to take a day or two to try using a new tool or library that could speed up your product (and you're not on a tight deadline), it's easy to say, "Sure, give it a shot." If, on the other hand, she wants to do something like launch a product that you're going to have to support for the next 10 years, you'll likely want to give it a bit more thought. Really good leaders have a good sense for when something can be undone.

Imposter Phenomenon

Much has been written about the so-called "imposter syndrome" or "imposter phenomenon,"[13] which according to Wikipedia is a *"psychological phenomenon in which people are unable to internalize their accomplishments. Despite external evidence of their competence, those with the*

---

13 First documented by Dr. Pauline Rose Clance, *http://paulineroseclance.com/impostor_phenomenon.html*.

syndrome remain convinced that they are frauds and do not deserve the success they have achieved."

We prefer the "phenomenon" nomenclature because, even though this may make you feel like a fraud who will be discovered at any time, the imposter phenomenon often drives you to work much harder and achieve goals that you might never have achieved otherwise.

This problem is extremely common in people new to management, especially those thrust into leadership positions (official or not) by necessity. The phenomenon is so widespread that we almost always get asked about it after our talks. *"I don't actually know what I'm doing,"* people will say, *"so what can I do to stop feeling like a phony?"* Our answer is that everyone feels like a phony at some point in their career; one could even argue that a little bit of insecurity makes us work harder and helps improve our success.

Ben likes to share the story of his parents' marriage. The night before they got married, they both got cold feet and admitted to each other that they had made a Terrible Mistake—but that it was clearly far too late to call off the wedding. So they made a pact to "fake it" for the wedding, play the stage role of happy newlyweds, and then maybe call things off a few days later. A couple of weeks later, they decided to try another month of marriage. And then the month after that, and the month after that. Eventually it became a running joke in their marriage. Every year on their anniversary they would say, "Let's give this trial another year, eh?"

Whatever sort of leadership you're involved in, the same "fake it till you make it" technique tends to work very well. When Ben first got asked to manage a large team, a similar script went through his mind: *"You want me to own this project? That's crazy, but OK, I guess I'll pretend to be a leader for a while."* Then every year at performance-review time, he'd look back at his success and and say, *"Yeah, I guess I'll keep pretending a bit longer—seems to be going well!"*

People Are Like Plants

Fitz's wife is the youngest of six children, and her mother was faced with the difficult task of figuring out how to raise six *very different* children, each of whom needed different things. Fitz asked his mother-in-law how she managed this (see what we did there?), and she responded that kids are like plants: some are like cactuses and need little water but lots of sunshine, others are like African violets and need diffuse light and moist soil, and still others are like tomatoes and will truly excel if you give them a little fertilizer. If you have six kids and give each one the same amount of water, light, and fertilizer, they'll all get equal treatment, but the odds are good that *none* of them will get what they actually *need*.

And so your team members are also like plants: some need more light, and some need more water (and some need more bullshit, er, fertilizer). It's your job as their leader to figure out who needs what and to then give it to them.

Take a look at this matrix:

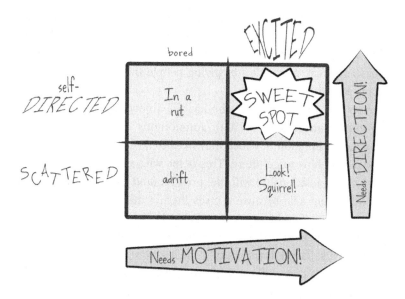

To get all of your team members into the sweet spot, you need to motivate the ones who fall into the "In a rut" portion of the matrix, and provide stronger direction to those who are in the "Look! Squirrel!" portion. Of course, those who are "adrift" need both motivation *and* direction. So, instead of water and sunlight, you need to provide team members with a combination of motivation and direction to make them happy and productive. And you don't want to give them too much of either—because if they don't need motivation or direction and you try giving it to them, you're just going to annoy them.

Giving direction is fairly straightforward—it requires a basic understanding of what needs to be done, some simple organizational skills, and enough coordination to break it down into manageable tasks. With those tools in hand you can provide enough guidance for an engineer in need of directional help (OK, there's more to it, but we covered a lot of that earlier in the chapter). Motivation, however, is a bit more sophisticated and merits some explanation.

Intrinsic Versus Extrinsic Motivation

There are two types of motivation: extrinsic, which originates from outside forces (such as monetary compensation), and intrinsic, which comes from within. In his book *Drive*,[14] Dan Pink explains that the way to make people the happiest and most productive isn't to motivate them extrinsically (e.g., throw piles of cash at them), but rather to work to increase their *intrinsic* motivation. Dan claims you can increase intrinsic motivation by giving people three things: autonomy, mastery, and purpose.[15]

A person has *autonomy* when she has the ability to act on her own without someone micromanaging her.[16] With autonomous employees, you might give them the general direction in which they need to take the product, but leave it up to them to decide how to get there. This helps with motivation not only because they have a closer relationship with the product (and likely know better than you how to build it), but also because it gives them a much greater sense of ownership of the product. The bigger their stake is in the success of the product, the greater their interest is in seeing it succeed.

Mastery in its basest form simply means you need to give someone the opportunity to learn new skills and improve existing skills. Giving ample opportunities for mastery not only helps to motivate people, but also makes them better over time, which makes for stronger teams.[17] An employee's skills are like the blade of a knife: you may spend tens of thousands of dollars to find people with the sharpest skills for your team, but if you "use" that knife for years without sharpening it, you will wind up with a dull knife that is inefficient, and in some cases useless. Ample opportunities for team members to learn new things and master their craft will keep them sharp, efficient, and effective.

Of course, all the autonomy and mastery in the world isn't going to help motivate someone if she's doing work for no reason at all, which is why you need to give her work *purpose*. Many people work on products that have great significance, but they are kept at arm's length from the positive effects their products may have on their company, their customers, or even the world. Even in cases where the product may have a much smaller impact, you can motivate your team by seeking the reason for their efforts and making this reason clear to them. If you can help them to see this purpose in their work, you'll see a tremendous

---

14 As we mentioned earlier in this chapter, see also Dan's fantastic TED talk on this subject.

15 This assumes that the people in question are being paid well enough that income is not a source of stress.

16 Of course, this assumes that you have people on your team who don't need micromanagement.

17 Of course, it also means they're more valuable and marketable employees, so it's easier for them to pick up and leave you if they're not enjoying their work. See the pattern in "Track Happiness" on page 72.

increase in their motivation and productivity.[18] One manager we know keeps a close eye on the email feedback the company gets for its product (one of the "smaller-impact" products), and whenever she sees a message from a customer talking about how the company's product has helped the customer personally or helped the customer's business, she immediately forwards it to the engineering team. This not only motivates the team, but also frequently inspires them to think about ways they can make their product even better.

Final Thoughts

Regardless of whether you ever intend to lead a team, we hope this chapter has helped you understand what it takes to be a good team leader and dispelled some of the myths about what a leader does for a team. Even if you're resolute in your commitment to never be a leader, it's good to be familiar with the concepts laid out in this chapter because they can help you understand why the leader of *your* team does what she does, regardless of whether she's good at her job or terrible at it. Take a moment to look at your team and see which of these patterns and antipatterns your team leader applies to make your team succeed (or fail), and you'll have a more concrete understanding of what makes your team tick.

But understanding the team and leader you work with every day is only one aspect of working with other people—crossing paths with someone outside your team can be even more challenging, especially if this person is out to sabotage your team. We call these "poisonous people," and we discuss them in the following chapter.

---

18 *http://bit.ly/task_significance*

4

Dealing with Poisonous People

As the opening quote of our book suggests, the hardest part of creative work is *people*.

Up until now, we've taken an introspective approach. We began with an examination of your own private behaviors and how to focus them on the principles of humility, respect, and trust (HRT). We then explored ways to build a communicative team culture around these concepts. In the preceding chapter, we explained how to mold yourself into an effective leader of such a team, should the need arise.

In the second half of this book we're going to shift gears and start looking outward. How does your team interact with people *outside* your immediate group? There are almost always folks wishing to join or collaborate with your team. There are issues in dealing with the politics of your larger organization. And, of course, you need to have a plan for dealing with the most important outsiders of all: the users of your software!

In this chapter, we'll discuss the importance of preventing destructive outsiders from trashing the cooperative culture your team has worked hard to build. Perhaps more importantly, we'll also talk about how to deal with poisonous people already on your team.

Defining "Poisonous"

We've already reviewed the importance of building a solid, communicative team culture. We spent most of the time talking about what a good culture should include: things like consensus-based development, high-quality code, code reviews, and an environment where people feel comfortable enough to try new things and to fail fast.

Just as important is the need to talk about what your culture should *not* include. If you're trying to build a highly efficient, fast-moving team, it's important to focus on what you *don't* want. While brilliant engineers can make your team faster and more efficient, certain antibehaviors can make your team slower and less efficient, and make your company a less comfortable place to work—and eventually erode the bonds that hold the team together.

When we first began speaking about the social challenges of software development, we came up with a presentation titled "How to Deal with Bad Eggs." A conference chair suggested we rename the talk to "How Projects Survive Poisonous People," with the hope that a more sensational title would draw a bigger audience. And he was right: we gave the presentation over and over at different conferences to standing-room-only crowds. It's not just the negativity of a word like *poisonous* that attracted people, but the fact that everyone seems to have some sort of personal experience in dealing with irritating people. The talks would almost always turn into a group therapy session, with audience members swapping war stories and seeking advice.

But there's a danger here. In general, it's not healthy to spend your time stewing in an ocean of negativity—it tends to eat you up and can create more conflicts in the long run.[1] The term *poisonous person* is a nasty label and automatically creates a dividing line between "us" (the good guys) and "them" (those nasty jerks). There's a better way to think about the problem. Instead of running your team as an elite fraternity with a mission to "repel mean people," it's healthier to create a culture that simply refuses to tolerate certain negative behaviors. It's the *behaviors* you want to filter out, not particular individuals. It's naïve to think of individuals as purely good or bad; it's more constructive and practical to identify and reprimand the intolerable behaviors.

For now, we'll continue to use the term *poisonous person* as a simplifying piece of rhetoric, one that refers to a person who isn't behaving well. In practice, though, this is not a term you'd want to use in everyday conversations!

Fortifying Your Team

Recall our yeast metaphor: how a team culture grows from an important starter culture. The biggest single influence on the long-term culture of your team is the team you start with, and if the founding team doesn't establish a strong enough

---

1 Yoda would probably have something to say here about avoiding the Dark Side.

culture, strains of other cultures will overgrow it. If your starter team builds a strong sense of acceptable and unacceptable behaviors, these expectations will endure.

The two of us have spent a lot of time in the world of open source projects, and our own experiences jibe with this idea pretty strongly.

The project we were most involved with—Subversion—was started by a very small group of people. They had a lot of humility and naturally trusted and respected one another. After 15-plus years, the project has gone through at least three or four generations of participants (the founders are mostly gone), and yet the same culture persists—everyone is kind, is polite, and expects that same behavior from everyone else. The culture perpetuates not just because of high standards, but because cultures tend to be *self-selecting*. Nice people tend to be attracted to existing nice communities.

Self-selection can easily work in the other direction as well. When a team is started by a group of angry jerks, the effort tends to attract more and more individuals of the same sort. Certain projects that we won't mention here (like the Linux kernel community) are keen examples of this—full of endless bickering and chest thumping. Yes, the team may get a lot of work done, but the overall *efficiency* of its operation is doubtful. How much more work would get done if so much energy weren't being spent on personal attacks? How much potential contribution is lost because polite people are being driven away at the front door?

We bring up this topic again because you need to understand what's at stake: poisonous people are a direct threat to your high-functioning team. If you allow bad behaviors to persist, not only does your productivity decrease, but you may also find your culture slowly changing for the worse. The best defense is to fortify your culture through a strong set of best practices and procedures. We covered them in Chapter 2, but here's a quick refresher:

- Have a visible mission statement, to keep you focused on both your goals and nongoals.

- Establish proper etiquette around email discussions. Keep archives, get newcomers to read them, and prevent filibustering by noisy minorities.

- Document all history: not just code history, but also design decisions, important bug fixes, and prior mistakes.

- Collaborate effectively. Use version control, keep code changes small and reviewable, and spread the "bus factor" around to prevent territoriality.

- Have clear policies and procedures around fixing bugs, testing, and releasing software.

- Streamline the barrier to entry for newcomers.

- Rely on consensus-based decisions, but also have a fallback process for resolving conflicts when consensus can't be reached.

The bottom line is that the more ingrained these best practices are, the more intolerant of poisonous behavior your community will be. When troublemakers arrive, you'll be ready.

Identifying the Threat

If you're going to defend your team against poisonous people, the first thing you need to do is to understand exactly what constitutes a threat and when you should become concerned.

What's specifically at risk is your team's *attention* and *focus*.

Attention and focus are the scarcest resources you have. The bigger the team, the more capacity the team has to focus on building things and solving interesting problems—but it's always a finite amount. If you don't actively protect these things, it's easy for poisonous people to disrupt your team's flow. Your team ends up bickering, distracted, and emotionally drained. Everyone ends up spending all their attention and focus on things *other* than creating a great product.

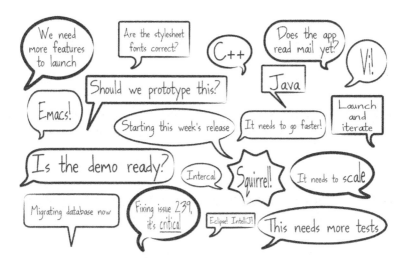

Meanwhile, one has to wonder: what does a poisonous person look like? To defend yourself, you need to know what to look out for.

In our experiences, it's rare to find people who are deliberately being malicious (i.e., are trying to be jerks on purpose). We call such people "trolls" and typically ignore them. Most people who behave badly, however, either don't realize it or simply don't care. It's more an issue of ignorance or apathy, rather than malice. Most of the bad behaviors boil down to a simple lack of HRT.

Here are some classic signals and patterns to watch for. Whenever we see these patterns, we talk about "flipping the bozo bit" on the person—that is, we make a mental note that the person is consistently exhibiting poisonous behaviors and that we should be extremely careful in dealing with her.

LACK OF RESPECT FOR OTHER PEOPLE'S TIME

There are certain people out there who simply are unable to figure out what's going on in a project. Their damage is most often in the form of wasting the team's time. Rather than spending a few minutes of their own time reading fundamental project documentation, mission statements, FAQs, or the latest email discussion threads, they repeatedly distract the entire team with questions about things they could easily figure out on their own.

In the Subversion project, we once had a participant who decided to use the main developer discussion forum as a sounding board for his daily stream of consciousness. Charlie made no actual code contribution. Instead, every two or three hours, he'd send out his latest daydreams and brainstorms. There would inevitably be multiple responses explaining why his ideas were incorrect, impossible, already in progress, previously discussed, and/or already documented. To make things worse, Charlie even started answering questions from drive-by users, and answering them *incorrectly*. Core contributors had to repeatedly correct his replies. It took us quite a while to realize that this affable, enthusiastic participant was in fact poisonous and draining our collective energy. Later in this chapter we'll talk about how we dealt with the situation.

EGO

Perhaps *ego* isn't the perfect word here, but we're using the term to describe anyone who is incapable of accepting a consensus decision, listening to or respecting other points of view, or reaching compromises. This person will typically reopen discussions that have been long settled (and documented in email archives) because she wasn't around to participate in the decision. The person won't read or think about the history at all, demanding that the debate be replayed just for her sake. She will often make sweeping claims about the project's success, claiming that doom is imminent unless she gets her way.

The Subversion project had a notable episode in which an intelligent programmer showed up on the email list one day and declared that the entire product was ill-designed. He had seen the light, had radical ideas about how things should work, and insisted that the entire project start over from scratch. He even helpfully volunteered to lead the reboot himself. Without his leadership, he proclaimed that complete failure was looming just around the corner.

An entire week was wasted while the project founders endlessly argued with this person and defended their original design decisions. A huge amount of attention and focus was lost. It became clear that this person wasn't willing to compromise or integrate any of his ideas into the current product, and the product (which was already in beta and being used in the wild) wasn't about to start over. At some point we simply had to walk away from the debate and get back on track. Ironically, years later, this person's predictions turned out to be correct on many levels, but that didn't stop Subversion from becoming wildly successful anyway—at least in corporate software development. The point here isn't about who is right or wrong, but whether a disagreement is guaranteed to come to a conclusion and whether it's worthwhile to keep a debate going. Never stop asking yourself those sorts of questions; at some point you need to decide when it's time to cut your losses and move on.

ENTITLEMENT

Anytime you have a visitor who *demands* that something be done, your alarm should go off. Something is wrong with a person who puts all her energy into complaining about the inadequacies of the software but is unwilling to directly contribute in any way.

This sense of entitlement sometimes bleeds into troll-like behavior. While running Google's Project Hosting service, we once had a project owner ask us to ban a user for obscene behavior. The open source project, a video game emulator, didn't work properly for his favorite video game. The user started by filing a rather rude bug in the issue tracker. The project developers politely explained why the game didn't work yet, and why it was unlikely to be fixed for a good while. This answer was unacceptable to the user, who began to harass the developers daily. He would open bug after bug with the same complaint. He started adding comments to *other* bugs saying what "idiots" the developers were for refusing to fix his problem. His language became increasingly obscene over time, despite repeated warnings from the developers and Google administrators. Regardless of all our efforts to eliminate his destructive behavior, he steadfastly refused to change, so we were eventually forced—as a last resort—to ban him entirely.

IMMATURE OR CONFUSING COMMUNICATION

The person doesn't use her real name. Instead, you'll see only childish nicknames like "SuperCamel," "jubjub89," or "SirHacksalot." To make things worse, often the person will have different nicknames in different media—one name for email, a different one for instant messaging, and perhaps a different one for code submissions. In extreme cases, you'll see these people communicating in lolspeak, 1337speak, ALL CAPS, or with excessive punctuation!??!1!!1!!

PARANOIA

As seen in the earlier example, sometimes an inappropriate sense of entitlement leads directly into open hostility toward a project. Many times we see it escalate into complete paranoia. When an existing team disagrees with the visitor, the poisonous person will sometimes start to throw accusations of a "cabal" and conspiracy. It's amusing to imagine that the project team finds him so important that they'd go through the effort of conspiring against the visitor. And if you already have an open and transparent culture of communication (as we pushed for in Chapter 2), this makes the accusation all the more hilarious, since every conversation is already a public record. The recommendation here is to not even bother responding to such charges. By the time the poisonous person goes this far over the edge, anything you say will only dig yourself a deeper hole in his mind, so why bother saying anything at all? It's time to get back to the important work of making things.

PERFECTIONISM

On the surface, perfectionists don't seem dangerous at all. Sure, there may be a touch of odd obsessive-compulsive behavior now and then, but usually the person is humble, polite, respectful, and a good listener. He seems stuffed full of happy HRT and good intentions. What's the problem, then? The problem is the threat of paralysis.

Let's look at a person we've worked with in the past. Patrick was a brilliant engineer. He had great design chops, wrote high-quality code and tests, and was easy to get along with. Unfortunately, when it came time to design new software, he could spend the rest of his life tweaking and improving his design. He was never satisfied with the plans and seemingly was never ready to start coding. While he certainly had good points and excellent insights into the problems we were trying to solve, the rest of the team ended up becoming immensely frustrated; it became clear that we were never actually going to write any code. Several of us on the project deliberated quite a bit on what to do about this. On the one hand, Patrick was a huge help to our team. On the other hand, he was preventing us from making forward progress as a group. Every time we'd begin to code he'd politely veto and point out potential theoretical problems that could matter in the distant future. He was paralyzing us without realizing it. We'll talk about how we resolved this in the next section.

Repelling the Poison

We don't advocate throwing people out of a community just because they're being antisocial or rude. As we mentioned earlier, it's not healthy to create a clique focused on "us" (the nice people) versus "them" (the mean people). In our prior examples we didn't focus on booting the person, but rather on booting the *behavior*. Make it clear that bad behaviors will not be tolerated. If, after repeated warnings, the behavior doesn't change, only then does it makes sense to consider formal rejection.

Concentrating your effort on removing toxic behavior is often enough to turn an intelligent (although perhaps socially awkward) person into a productive member of your team. A few years ago we had a team member who was an excellent engineer but had an annoying habit of accidentally insulting teammates. Rather than just ejecting him from the community, one of us pulled him aside and asked him if he was aware that his words were alienating people. He seemed somewhat surprised that this was happening and didn't exactly understand why his actions were having this effect. But he agreed that it would be worthwhile to try to temper his actions in the interest of being a better team member. And everything worked out perfectly. He changed his behavior, and the problem was resolved. Not every anecdote ends in exile!

OK, so you've identified a poisonous person. Perhaps there's someone distracting and draining your team's energy right now. How do you deal effectively with the situation? Here are some useful strategies.

REDIRECT THE ENERGY OF PERFECTIONISTS

Once a good-enough solution is found for the original problem, point the perfectionist to a different problem that still needs attention.

In the case of Subversion's perfectionist, this strategy worked well. Eventually, we reached a point where we took Patrick aside and said, "OK, we're just going to start working from this design as it stands now, and see what happens. Hopefully you'll be able to help us navigate around any problems that crop up down the road." To our surprise, Patrick was OK with this and instead moved on to a different subject as the object of his obsession. No feelings were hurt either way, and Patrick kept contributing to the overall effort.

There's an old saying to not let "the perfect be the enemy of the good," and in your quest to create a high-performing team, you need to be just as vigilant about avoiding perfectionism as you are about calling out more obvious disruptive behaviors.

This trick of redirecting energy also works on the overly entitled people who spend more time complaining and criticizing than helping out. It's tempting to respond to such a person with a standard "patches welcome" remark—the open source community's euphemistic version of telling someone to put up or shut up. Instead, try getting him to take an interest in formally testing the software and pointing out regressions. It allows him to keep complaining, but in a useful way.

DON'T FEED THE ENERGY CREATURE

This is an old adage from Usenet.[2] In particular, this works best against deliberate trolls—people who are purposely trying to get a rise out of you or your team. The more you respond, the more the troll feeds off your energy, and the more time you've wasted. The simple silent treatment often works best. Regardless of how much you're dying to deliver that one-line zinger that'll put him in his place, resist the urge. When the person realizes nobody's paying attention, he typically loses interest and just leaves. Note that it often takes quite a bit of willpower to not respond. Stay strong!

DON'T GET OVERLY EMOTIONAL

Even if the person isn't deliberately trolling, it's all too easy to get defensive. When somebody accuses you of making a bad design decision or of conspiracy, or simply wastes your time by asking too many questions whose answers are obvious, it's easy to get upset. Remember that your job is to build great things, not to appease every visitor or repeatedly justify your existence. The stronger your emotions are, the more likely you are to waste hours or days writing passionate replies to someone who doesn't deserve such attention. Choose your battles care-

---

2 Which may itself refer to that original *Star Trek* episode, "Day of the Dove," in which negative emotions fed an energy creature. Kirk and his Klingon counterpart Kang ordered their men to stop feeding the energy creature, and it departed from the *Enterprise*. See, it all comes back to *Star Trek*.

fully and keep calm. Carefully decide who's worth replying to, and who you'll let be.

LOOK FOR FACTS IN THE BILE

Continuing on with the theme of staying clear of too much emotion, a corollary is to actively look for facts. If someone is complaining, listen carefully. Always start by giving the person the benefit of the doubt, despite the angry or rude language. Does the person have a real point? Is there something to learn from the person's experience, or is there an idea worth responding to? Very often the answer is "yes"—that despite a poisonous person's vitriolic prose, some wisdom really is buried in there. Always bring the argument back to a technical discussion.[3]

Our favorite example of this is the day we got a rancorous email from a well-known leader of the open source community. It was a bug report of sorts, but on the surface it was more like a rant about the team's overall intelligence. The post was chock-full of slander and hyperbole, and seemed intended to inflame the team rather than to get the bug fixed. One of our team members, however, responded to the report with just a few specific questions, focusing only on the bug. The bug reporter replied with more clarification, but still it was wrapped in over-the-top venom. Our team member continued to completely ignore the insults, investigated the issue, and replied with a simple "Thanks for the bug report, I see how to fix the problem—we'll release a patch soon."

We were immensely proud of the way our team member handled the situation. Remaining utterly calm and fact-driven only made the original poster seem like more of a lunatic as the conversation progressed. By the end of the exchange, the bug reporter had lost all credibility with his audience and no longer had any interest in hanging around.

REPEL TROLLS WITH NICENESS

To take the preceding approach (of remaining cool-headed and factual) even further, sometimes it's possible to scare people away just by being too kind! Here's an actual chat transcript from the Subversion IRC channel:

---

3 For more on this subject, see Norman Kerth's "The Retrospective Prime Directive," in his book *Project Retrospectives* (Dorset House).

harry: Subversion sucks. This is quite a nuisance.

sussman: If you need help, then ask.

harry: I want to cvs someone's files. No, I just want to gripe. But this person is hung up on this thing called Subversion so he has svn instead of cvs.

sussman: So get an svn client and checkout his sources.

harry: So I go and download this Subversion thing...can you configure make make install Subversion like you can cvs? Of course not. I blame him more than the subversion people.

*sussman: Just because **you** can't ./configure; make; make install doesn't mean there's a big widespread bug. People do that with the svn tarball every day.*

harry: I didn't say there was a bug.

sussman: Do you think we would have released the tarball if something that fundamental were broken?

*harry: I am just griping about this bozo. I just have to install expat or libxml. **sigh***

sussman: Those things are usually pre-installed on most systems.

sussman: Is this guy using an apache server? Perhaps you should just grab a binary.

harry: I don't know, he just says svn...

sussman: Which distro are you on?

harry: FreeBSD

sussman: Just cd into the ports tree and make the port.

harry: You people are ruining my rant...I came here looking for an argument...you are too helpful and friendly.

sussman: :-)

harry: When the hell do you come to an IRC channel and everyone tries to help you? Blah.

— Harry has quit

KNOW WHEN TO GIVE UP

Sometimes no matter how hard you try, you simply need to flip the bozo bit and move on. Even if you've already spent a lot of attention and focus trying to correct bad behaviors, you need to know how to recognize a lost cause.

Let's return to our story about Charlie, the friendly philosopher who was posting far too often to the Subversion email list. Eventually we did an analysis of the email discussions and discovered that this participant had grown into the third most frequent poster over the course of two months; the first and second most frequent posters were core project contributors, and 70% of their posts were spent *replying to Charlie!* Clearly our energy and focus were being sucked away, despite no ill will from Charlie himself. Our final solution was to privately email him and (politely) ask him to stop posting so often. It was a difficult conversation to have, mainly because he was unable to see the amount of disruption he was causing. After a few more weeks without a significant behavioral change, one of us actually had a long (and even more difficult) discussion with him over the phone where we asked him to stop posting altogether. He ultimately withdrew as requested, a bit sad and confused, but respectful of the team's wishes. Everyone felt a little guilty about it because he never quite understood the harm he was causing, but everyone also felt it was the right thing to do. It was a delicate situation to resolve, but we used a great deal of HRT to keep things civil and appropriate.

FOCUS ON THE LONG TERM

The path to a successful project is lined by thousands of distractions. If there's a common theme in dealing with the distraction of poisonous people, it's that it's all too easy to get caught up in the immediate drama of a situation. If you're witnessing what you think may be poisonous behavior, you need to ask yourself two critical questions:

- Despite the short-term loss of your team's attention and focus, *do you truly believe the project will still benefit in the long run?*
- Do you believe the conflict will ultimately resolve itself in a useful way?

If your answer to either of these questions is "no," you need to intervene to stop the behavior as soon as possible. It's easy to persuade ourselves that the short-term gain of tolerating poison is worth it, but it usually isn't: for example, somebody may be a great technical contributor but still exhibit poisonous behavior. There's a temptation to turn a blind eye to the behavior in order to benefit from the technical advancement. But be careful! A strong culture based on HRT is irreplaceable, while technical contributions are *definitely* replaceable. To quote a former teammate of ours:

> *I have several friends who know him to some degree. One of them said, "He often walks the fine line between genius and lunatic." The problem is, genius is such a commodity these days that it's not acceptable to be an eccentric anymore.*

> —*Greg Hudson*

Of course, Greg isn't talking about literal "genius" here; he's pointing out that the world is full of highly competent programmers. If you find one who's offensive or threatens your culture over the long term, it's best to wait for another one to come along.

We once encountered this sort of situation in the Subversion project. The team has a strict policy of not putting names into source code files (the very policy we discussed in Chapter 2!): we feel it creates unmanageable territoriality. People are afraid to change code if it has somebody else's name on it, and it keeps the bus factor artificially low. Instead, we allow the version control's history to credit people appropriately, and we keep a single top-level file with all the contributors' names in it.

One day a smart programmer showed up and volunteered to write a sizable new feature that was sorely needed. He submitted the code for review, and our main feedback was simply requesting that he remove his name from the top of the file—that we'd credit him in the same places as everyone else. He refused to do this, however, and the debate led to an impasse. In the end, the decision was made to reject his code and he left, taking his toys with him. Of course everyone was disappointed, but we didn't want to violate our policy (and dilute our culture) just to get the new feature sooner. A couple of months later, someone else ended up reimplementing the feature anyway.

To be explicit: *it's not worth compromising your culture for the short-term gains*—particularly if it's about a brilliant contributor who doesn't acknowledge the importance of HRT.

A Final Thought

This chapter discussed quite a number of scenarios, and after taking everything in it's easy to develop a deep sense of paranoia. Please remember that most of the world isn't overflowing with jerks. A friend of ours once noted, "Yeah, there are only a few crazy people out there; the Internet just makes it seems like they all live next door."

Or, as the saying from Robert J. Hanlon goes:

Never attribute to malice that which is adequately explained by stupidity.

We prefer to use the term *ignorance* rather than *stupidity*, but the idea is the same. As we mentioned in the beginning, it's naïve to think of people as Good or Bad. There are very few evil people out there trying to deliberately crush your culture—most of them are simply misinformed or misguided. Or perhaps they just want recognition and are too socially inept to fit in. Either way, your job isn't to cultivate condescension and lock out the less enlightened peasants from your project; rather, your job is to be intolerant of destructive behaviors and to be explicit about your expectations of HRT. It takes wisdom to understand the difference and real skill to carry it out.

5

The Art of Organizational Manipulation

So far we've shown you how to handle the human side of you and your team. We've reviewed the basic people skills required for leading a team and the hazards of dealing with the threat of poisonous people. In addition to these skills, you also need to understand how to navigate good and poisonous companies alike. Most people work in dysfunctional corporate bureaucracies and need to employ certain manipulative techniques to get things done effectively. Some people call this politics; others call it social engineering.

We call it organizational manipulation.

The Good, the Bad, and the Strategies

Big companies are complex mazes, and even the best require a GPS, a flashlight, and a dump truck full of breadcrumbs to navigate from one end of the company to the other.

First we'll cover how a team typically functions in an ideal company, and then we'll discuss the various ways a dysfunctional company can put up roadblocks to your team's success. We'll review strategies for getting things done in both kinds of companies, and lastly, if all else fails, we'll cover Plan B.

How Things Ought to Be

There are two levels of a properly functioning company: your manager, who you'll deal with most of the time, and the corporation beyond your manager, which includes knowledge workers, middle managers, executives, salespeople, lawyers, and so on.

THE IDEAL EMPLOYEE EXPERIENCE

If your manager is a servant leader who employs HRT and is truly interested in helping you succeed (see Chapter 3), there are a few simple things you can do to help make her job easier, and consequently make yourself more productive and a more valuable team member. Perhaps more importantly, they can make your job better and your career more successful.

Pursue extra responsibility as you're getting your work done. One of our favorite metaphors for this is the forest ranger who sends you, a junior ranger, into the forest to cut down a sick or damaged tree. If you're focused merely on the task at hand, you'll go into the forest, cut down the sick tree, and return triumphant. If, however, you're thinking about the bigger picture, you'll go into the forest, cut down the sick tree, and return with a map of all the other sick trees you encountered on your journey, along with a plan for efficiently cutting them down if the senior ranger agrees that this is the best plan of action. As a result of this kind of action, the next time the forest ranger has a task that requires that level of responsibility she'll likely give you the first shot at it. She'll do this not only because she knows you can do it, but because that's the path of least resistance—it's less work for her.

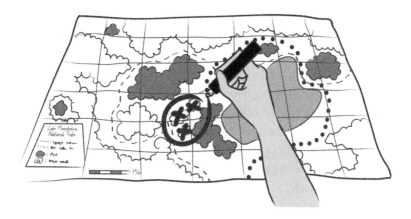

This kind of proactive, responsibility-seeking behavior reduces your manager's workload because she has one less thing to worry about, and it shows that you're capable of doing work beyond your current level. This also means you'll likely have to leave your comfort zone and try new things, and that's OK if you're on a team where you're encouraged to take risks and fail fast.

Take risks and don't fear failure. We talked a lot in Chapters 3 and 4 about the importance of taking risks and failing fast. In the presence of an enlightened manager, failing is a great way to learn quickly, discover the limits of what you can and can't do, and grow those limits over time. Our friend Steve Hayman, who travels a lot for work, has often said, "If you don't miss at least one flight a year, you're getting to the airport too early." This is a great metaphor for creating any sort of product: if you don't fail at least once a year, you're not taking enough risks. And like the pursuit of extra responsibility, taking risks is a way to show you're capable of bigger things.

If you don't take risks in your work, you'll have fewer failures, but you'll have fewer big successes as well. A good manager wants a team that's willing to push the envelope to see what they can and can't do (and to learn a lot in the process), and she'll provide a soft landing for when you fail. When you fail, take responsibility, don't seek to assign blame, and document what happened and what you can do to avoid that same failure again. Lather, rinse, repeat.

Act like an adult. Another recommendation in a long line of suggestions that seem glaringly obvious: you are responsible for teaching people how to act and how to treat you. Bad managers will frequently train their teams to act like children by squashing any initiative, responsibility, or rule breaking. If you've had one of these managers, you often come to expect this sort of treatment from all managers.

Question things that you're unsure about. If your manager makes a decision that you disagree with, don't be afraid to argue with her or question the premise upon which she made the decision. While this isn't a license to be an obstacle, being a "yes-man" isn't helpful to someone in a leadership position if you've got information or experience that she lacks.

Your manager is not clairvoyant: only rarely will you find a person in an organization who *over*communicates, so don't hesitate to update your team's leader on what you're doing before she asks you what's going on. Drop her a quick note when you hit an obstacle, score a victory, need something, or expect something. Not only is this a great way to make sure your manager knows what you're up to, but we've seen crafty engineers take this technique to the extreme as a way to deal with micromanagement: if your manager keeps checking in on you, proactively sending her an email at the same frequency with which she checks in on you is a surefire way to get her to back off.

These techniques work well when you're in the ideal organization, but what about when your organization is anything but ideal?

How Things Usually Are

Happy families are all alike; every unhappy family is unhappy in its own way.

—Leo Tolstoy, Anna Karenina[1]

There are innumerable ways in which the environment in your company can work to prevent you from succeeding, but they can usually be divided into two major categories: bad people and bad organizations.

---

1 See "Anna Karenina principle," http://en.wikipedia.org/wiki/Anna_Karenina_principle.

THE BAD MANAGER

It's hard to know where to start in describing the traits of a bad manager—entire movies and TV shows have been created solely to lampoon the bad managers of the world. Most of us have had at least one bad manager in our careers, and a bad manager can make life on even the greatest team a living hell, so we're going to cover just a few of the traits of a bad manager that typically affect engineers.

Fear of failure is one of the most common traits of bad managers. This insecurity tends to make them very conservative, which is antithetical to the work style of the typical engineer. If your manager doesn't want you to take risks, there is little opportunity for you to inject your own ideas into your product and you'll usually wind up implementing (by rote) the product someone else designed.[2]

Oftentimes the insecure manager will insist on inserting herself into any interaction you have with people outside your team, thereby preventing you from speaking directly to other teams without "going through the chain of command." This kind of manager will consider any direct contact you make with anyone outside your team—especially another manager—to be akin to mutiny or insubordination. If you need anything outside your team or their organization, this manager expects you to go through her, which allows her to elevate her importance and subordinate you, thus giving her more power.

Most of us grew up in school hearing the oft-repeated canard "knowledge is power." The bad manager is very much aware of this, but from a different angle: she wants to keep this power to herself and not share it with you, no matter how much it might help you to do your job. This manager hoards information and hides it from you as a way to make sure she can play a part in anything that involves that information, which not only keeps you from getting work done, but also helps her maintain her position of relevance and power no matter how much it slows down development.

---

2 Again, this is an acceptable way to write software; we just don't think it's a very interesting way for top-notch engineers to spend their time.

By hoarding information and requiring that they be a conduit for information and communication, bad managers are also able to take credit for your successes[3] and blame you for your failures (and sometimes, their failures as well). In many cases, this kind of bad manager sees your existence solely as a means to get herself promoted, and she doesn't care about your career, much less your team's happiness.

Our friend Susan had a terrible manager for a number of years, and her manager would often hand a new project off to Susan with no context, no information on how to get the project done, and no one to contact with questions. He would do this even if Susan had zero knowledge or context about the new task, because this forced her to rely on him for information as well as communication with other teams. Susan's manager didn't necessarily want Susan to fail: in fact, if he'd told Susan everything she needed to know about the project, it would have made Susan's life easier and more productive. On the other hand, he was most likely afraid that it would have been that much easier for her to circumvent him! Having the ability to directly contact relevant teams would have made them

---

3 Which is doubly frustrating because you managed to succeed in spite of their interference!

aware that Susan, and not her manager, was working on this project. Time and time again Susan would scramble to get up to speed on the new project, get it done, and then collapse, only to find out through the grapevine that her manager had taken credit for her work.

In stark contrast to the servant leader we discussed in Chapter 3, the bad manager wants to know what you've done for him lately. And those low performers on your team? They're not going anywhere as long as they don't grind your team to a screeching halt—it's too much work for the bad manager to deal with them. It boils down to this: is your manager serving you? Or are you serving your manager? It should *always* be the former.

THE OFFICE POLITICIAN

While we're big proponents of trusting people, or at the very least giving them the benefit of the doubt, trusting the office politician can be a seriously career-limiting move.

The office politician may be difficult to spot when you first meet him because he tends to be very good at managing relationships and dealing with people—he may be quite friendly at first. He usually does an exceptional job of managing up and an even better job of using his peers and subordinates as a means for self-promotion. He's quick to blame others, but even quicker to steal credit when given the opportunity. He's usually not directly confrontational, but instead prefers to tell you what you want to hear so that you'll think well of him. If he can't use you or manipulate you, he'll either ignore you or, if he sees you as a threat, try to undermine you. After you've worked with him for a while, it's easy to spot him: he spends more time *looking* impactful than actually *being* impactful.

We advise that you steer clear of the office politician: route around him where possible, but don't carelessly badmouth him to other people above him in the organization, because it's quite difficult to know who he has hoodwinked and who is wise to him. If you're the kind of person who is happy to keep your head down and focus on building interesting technology, you may want to rethink this strategy when there's an office politician around. If you don't put energy into getting promoted because you don't want to "play the game," you may find that the office politician gets promoted over you, in which case you've now got a bad manager *and* an office politician. See "Manipulating Your Organization" on page 108 for more on this.

THE BAD ORGANIZATION

As companies grow, they develop bureaucracy and processes in an effort to manage profit, reduce risk, increase predictability, and support the massive weight of the organization itself. Over time, this bureaucracy can grow to a point where it prevents the company from succeeding. As with bad managers, much has been written about bad organizations, so we're only going to review a few examples of organizational issues that most often affect individual contributors.

It's a simple fact that most companies are not engineering-focused. That is to say: engineers are a means to accomplish business goals that are typically not technical. This means the people running the company probably don't understand the technical underpinnings of their system, just the demands set upon them by the business, and so they wind up creating unrealistic demands on engineering. Even if a technically competent executive finds her way into this sort of company and fights to defend her organization, she'll frequently find herself replaced by someone who is willing to sacrifice the health and sanity of the employees to meet the needs of the business. Typically you'll see this directly in the form of unrealistic deadlines and lack of qualified technical people to get projects completed on time. You may have difficulty acquiring enough hardware to effectively run your product, or find your team spending weeks rewriting something when a hardware purchase costing only a few hundred dollars would have done the job. This is unfortunately typical of a company that doesn't value engineers and treats them like "work units" or "resources," giving them no voice in how the company operates.

The most egregiously bad organizations have ossified command and control structures that resemble fiefdoms. Years ago, our friend Terrence worked at a company that had strict rules on passing bugs between teams, and eventually another team created a bug that caused Terrence's product to run out of memory over the course of a few hours. Instead of emailing the team members who were responsible for this, or looking at their commit logs or source code, he stayed up all night reproducing the bug, gathering data, and building his case. Terrence sent this email to his manager, who sent the email to his director, who emailed the director of the team that created the bug. This director emailed that team's manager, who figured out who on his team was responsible for the software in question. More than 10 days later, Terrence found himself in a meeting with two managers, two directors, and three other engineers discussing the bug and whether they could get it fixed in time for their next launch. Sound absurd? Sadly, this sort of thing happens all the time. In contrast, during Fitz's first week at Google he found a typo in Gmail. He opened the source code, fixed the typo, then emailed a patch to the Gmail team, who thanked him heartily.

Many companies are filled with people who are obsessed with organizational hierarchy.[4] This results in endless power struggles, with managers often preventing engineers from transferring to another team in order to protect their own team from losing a valuable contributor—even when the right thing to do for both the company and the engineer is to let the transfer happen.

Has your company ever treated you like a naughty child? Are you unable to get to innocuous external websites due to an overzealous company firewall? Do you have to carefully account for every moment of your day with a detailed time-card? Some organizations will even go so far as to measure your productivity by meaningless (and usually wildly inaccurate) methods such as the number of lines of code you write every week.[5]

Still other organizations will breed employees who judge their success not by the number and quality of products they ship, but by the number of meetings they're invited to attend.

Lastly, your company might lack important things like focus, vision, or direction. This is often the result of too many masters, or "design by committee,"

---

4 In addition, in many dysfunctional companies, people are more concerned with their title than being productive or enjoying their job.

5 Shouldn't we get even more credit for deleting lines of code?

which results in conflicting orders being sent down to the rank and file. So you wind up moving in ever-tighter circles instead of in a coherent direction.

Many bad companies are guilty of these transgressions, and much, much more. Still, these companies are composed of people, and there are a number of tips and tricks you can put to bear to get people to help you out.

Manipulating Your Organization

This is a sparring program, similar to the programmed reality of the Matrix. It has the same basic rules, rules like gravity. What you must learn is that these rules are no different than the rules of a computer system. Some of them can be bent. Others can be broken. Understand? Then hit me if you can.

—Morpheus

Much like the sparring program, companies are made of rules: some of them can be bent, and others can be broken. If you focus on the way things *should* be in your organization, you'll usually find nothing but frustration and disappointment. Instead, acknowledge the way things *are*, and focus on navigating your organization's structure to find the mechanisms you can use to get things done and to carve out a happy place for yourself in your company. Whether you're in a good organization or a bad one, there are a number of strategies that we've found to be quite effective at getting things done.

"IT'S EASIER TO ASK FOR FORGIVENESS THAN PERMISSION"[6]

First and foremost, know what you can get away with in your organization— while asking for permission does give you an opportunity to push responsibility onto someone else, it also creates an opportunity for someone to tell you "no." It's important to know what you can get away with in your organization without explicitly getting approval from one of your superiors, but wherever possible, we advise you to do what you think is right for the company.

Even if you're prepared to beg for forgiveness, choose your battles wisely— every time you have to plead your case for something or go up against someone else in your company, you're spending your political capital. If you spend all your capital winning a bunch of battles that just don't matter, you're going to find that

---

6 Widely attributed to Admiral Grace Murray Hopper, coinventor of COBOL and an incredibly witty computer scientist.

you have nothing left in your account when it comes to the important things. Be strategic and fight for things either that matter or that you're pretty sure you have *some* chance of winning. Blowing all your capital on a battle you know you can't win is pointless, stressful, and career limiting for no good reason. For more details, see "Your Political Bank Account" on page 113.

If you do decide to go the "beg for forgiveness" route, it's useful to have colleagues and friends in your company that you can use as a sounding board for your ideas—especially your riskier ideas.

These people should have a good sense of what you can and can't get away with in the company as well as which ideas just won't fly.

When someone in marketing suggested that Fitz raise awareness of his Data Liberation team among the executives at Google, Fitz bounced an idea off his sounding-board colleagues: give Data Liberation–branded bolt cutters and locked boxes of swag (with the keys locked inside, of course) to the execs. He decided to go ahead with it and it was a big hit. A few years later, when Fitz was contemplating printing up some, shall we say, "off-color" swag, the same sounding board expressed some concern that the plan was too risky and Fitz decided to nix that plan. If you're going to act without asking permission, it's good to trust your instincts, but a second opinion from a trusted source is invaluable.

IF YOU CAN'T TAKE THE PATH, MAKE THE PATH

Another strategy for making change in a company is to find ways to get your ideas accepted at a grassroots level. If you can get enough people to buy into your idea or use a particular product, it will often be too late for the bureaucracy to squash you, and management will be forced to notice and either accept it or act against it (which costs them, yep, you guessed it, political capital!). This is a strategy that many engineers used for years, for example, to sneak open source tools into their daily workflow in order to make their lives a lot more pleasant.

Persuasion by proxy

If you're trying to persuade someone, a great way to increase your chances of success is to find several people who agree with you and get *them* to drop your idea (or proposal or request) in a conversation with that person. Even if your target is totally aware of what's going on, basic human psychology dictates that she'll give more weight to the idea because it's hitting her from multiple directions and not just from you.

Ideas in particular are fascinating things: they can go a long way if you don't care who gets the credit! Sometimes you'll find that people will spread an idea only if they can take credit for the idea as their own, so you need to decide what's more important: that you get the credit, or that the idea spreads. Despite the fact that it may pain you to hear your words coming out of another (perhaps despised) person's mouth, it's often the most effortless way for an idea to travel. We've seen this happen time and time again in companies large and small: the lofty concepts and ideas coming from an executive's mouth originate from someone in her organization. Think about the broad audience that your idea—which would otherwise go unheard—can reach in this case!

Just as with individuals, eliminating bad habits in a company is difficult. One of Ben's early teachers used to have a saying: "It's impossible to simply stop a bad habit; you need to *replace* it with a good habit." Anyone who's ever tried to quit smoking is intimately familiar with this phenomenon. Corporations are the same way—if you're going to successfully eliminate a bad habit, find a better one to replace it. Don't like a certain weekly meeting? Replace it with a different kind of meeting or alternate (more effective) ritual. Don't like a useless reporting process? Don't complain about it; write a useful one that's too compelling to ignore. Once you've found a good replacement habit, you need to overcome the inertia of change aversion, so we recommend offering to "try" your new ritual for a few weeks. This makes the new thing seem less permanent, less scary, and if it turns out that everyone likes the new ritual, by the time your "trial" period is over, they've forgotten that it was a trial in the first place.

LEARN TO MANAGE UPWARD

Whether you're a manager or an individual contributor, you need to spend some of your time managing upward. By this we mean you need to try to ensure that both your manager and the people outside your team are not only aware of what you're doing, but are aware that you're doing it well. Some people find this mode of "selling yourself" distasteful, and it may remain so, but the benefits of doing this are huge.

As we'll mention in Chapter 6, you need to underpromise and overdeliver whenever possible. We're not advocating that you sandbag all your estimates and pad out your deadlines, but wherever you can, try to avoid promising things that you can't deliver, even if it means saying "no" more often than you'd like. If you constantly miss deadlines or drop features, other people in the company will have less of a reason to trust you and will most likely pass over you when they're looking for someone to get something done.

We recommend that you focus your energies on *launching products* over just about everything else. Shipping things gives you credibility, reputation, and political capital more than just about anything else in a company. Launching your product is a high-visibility event that shows you're accomplishing something. As tempting as it might be to spend a ton of time cleaning up your code base and refactoring things, we've learned from experience that if you dedicate more than half of your time to this kind of defensive work, it's hardly valued at all by anyone outside of your team, including your superiors. You will then find yourself in the somewhat embarrassing position of having almost nothing (politically) important to show for your time.[7] This is not only a good way to get no recognition, but also a good way to get your product canceled.

"Offensive" Versus "Defensive" Work

When Ben first became a manager, it seemed like his team's productivity was being crushed under a mountain of accrued technical debt. He decided that the team's top priority was to spend a long time doing nothing but paying back this debt. His superiors gave a cursory nod to this plan and the work began. Things didn't go well. Despite the prior approval,

---

7 We're not saying that preventing future problems is unimportant, just that it's considerably more difficult to impress people outside your team with that sort of work.

Ben's manager began to get annoyed and impatient after a few months—why was the team getting "nothing done"? Ben's team was actually quite productive and he tried to show the enormous amount of debt that had been paid back. But it turns out there's just no way this sort of work can impress someone; at an emotional level it's just fundamentally boring.

After this bad experience, Ben began to categorize all work as either "offensive" or "defensive." *Offensive* work is typically effort toward new user-visible features—shiny things that are easy to show outsiders and get them excited about, or things that noticeably advance the appeal of a product (e.g., improved UI, faster response times). *Defensive* work is effort aimed at the long-term health of a product (e.g., code refactoring, feature rewrites, schema changes, data migration, or improved emergency monitoring). Defensive activities make the product more maintainable, stable, and reliable. And yet, despite the fact that they're absolutely critical, you *get no political credit* for doing them. If you spend all your time on them, people perceive your product as holding still. And to make wordplay on an old maxim: "Perception is nine-tenths of the law."

We now have a handy rule we live by: a team should never spend more than one-third to one-half of its time and energy on defensive work, no matter how much technical debt there is. Any more time spent is a recipe for political suicide.

LUCK AND THE FAVOR ECONOMY

Regardless of the kind of company you work in, believe it or not, it's not that hard to create a sort of luck for yourself. Richard Wiseman, author of *The Luck Factor*,[8] wrote about an experiment he performed to test the ability of people to spot chance opportunities:[9]

> I gave both lucky and unlucky people a newspaper, and asked them to look through it and tell me how many photographs were inside. On average, the unlucky people took about two minutes to count the photographs, whereas the lucky people took just seconds. Why? Because the second page of the newspaper contained the message: "Stop counting.

---

8 Published by Miramax (ISBN: 978-1401359416).

9 *http://bit.ly/luck_skill*

There are 43 photographs in this newspaper." This message took up half of the page and was written in type that was more than 2in high. It was staring everyone straight in the face, but the unlucky people tended to miss it and the lucky people tended to spot it.

He then goes on to note that lucky people "are skilled at creating and noticing chance opportunities." We think the same tenet applies to creating opportunities in companies: if you perform your job to the letter of the law and focus only on getting your own work done to the exclusion of all else, there will be few chance opportunities for you. If you help others get their jobs done when given the chance, even when it's not part of your job, there's no guarantee (nor should there be a "tit for tat" expectation) that they'll return the favor, but many people will gladly repay the favor in the future if given the chance.

YOUR POLITICAL BANK ACCOUNT

Every company has a gray-market favor economy that lives outside the org chart, and those favors are one of the main things that you can use to fill up your political bank account. There's usually something you can quickly and easily do that benefits your company but is someone else's job, and if you keep your eyes open for the chance to do these things (in many cases, someone will come right out and ask you to do something for them), you earn a bit of credit for your bank account in this favor economy. Think of these credits as a series of small bets: some will never pay you back, others will pay even money, and still others will pay *enormous* dividends. It's hard to know which bets will pay off, but one thing that will pay off over time is that people will remember you as the person who helped them out in a jam. Later on, when you're in a jam and you give them a call, they're going to be considerably more likely—even eager—to help you out than if you gave them a big fat "not my job" response when they came looking for help. Even if you never get "paid back" you'll often learn something new in the process of helping someone, and it feels good to help other people, so what do you have to lose other than a little time and effort?

This same political bank account is what you'll tap when you need to ask a favor of someone else in the company. It may be that you need someone to do something for you, or you do something that steps on someone else's toes, or you even just disagree with someone else in your company. It's incredibly useful to develop an awareness of when you're gaining political capital, and when you're spending it. If you fail to develop this awareness, there's a good chance that your account will be drained before you know it, leaving you powerless in your organization (and your career).

One of the most interesting things about the favor economy is that your bank account doesn't just empty out when you leave a job or a company—you'll frequently be able to call on folks at your company for a hand even after you've left. This is all the more reason that you should never burn bridges when you leave a company, no matter how tempting it might seem at the time.[10]

GET PROMOTED TO A POSITION OF SAFETY

If you're like most engineers, you expect a logical promotion process where all it should take to get promoted is to excel at your job. Unfortunately, this world exists only in the most enlightened companies. In most companies you need to put some amount of effort into "playing the promotion game" to get yourself promoted (usually *in addition* to excelling at your job).

---

10 Most industries are a lot smaller than you think, and people talk more than you think, so the person you stick it to today might very well be the one who kills your job application 10 years from now. Unless you're planning to move to a desert island to take up basket weaving, burning bridges will almost always be a costly mistake. Friends come and go...enemies accumulate.

If you're happy with your job, your salary, and your team, you might choose to not play the promotion game and settle into your job at whatever title and job level you're already at. This can leave you vulnerable in many situations—for example, your company reorganizes and you get shuttled to a new team, you get a bad manager, or you wind up under the thumb of the office politician.

The higher in the organization you can get (either as an individual contributor or as a manager), the more control you'll have over your destiny inside the company. Putting a modicum of effort toward getting promoted when you're comfortable in your position is a great way to invest in your security and happiness when something bad happens to your company or team. Keep track of your accomplishments and use them in your self-assessment. Update your résumé[11] and share it with your manager or promotion committee. Read up on the promotion process and talk to your manager about what boxes you need to tick off to get promoted, and methodically work to tick off every box. Even if getting promoted is subjective and nondeterministic, there's a lot you can do to increase the odds in your favor.

---

11 Contrary to our general advice in this book, your résumé is *exactly* the place where you want to exercise your personal ego and eschew humility. While we discourage dipping into the realm of fiction on your résumé, it's one place where you should toot your own horn, and toot it loudly.

SEEK POWERFUL FRIENDS

Every company has a "shadow" org chart that is unwritten but through which power and influence flow. There are only a few different types of people who make up the nodes in this graph.

Connectors are people who know people in every corner of the organization, and if they don't know someone on a team, they can find the right person for you. Sometimes getting something done is just a matter of finding the right person to speak to, and the connector can help you find that person.

Old-timers may not have a high rank or fancy title, but they typically carry a lot of institutional knowledge and wield a lot of influence just because they've been around for a long time. These are great people to go to when you're trying to understand why the organization works in a certain way, or if you need a supporter that a lot of people respect.

People most often talk about this in jest, but *administrative assistants* wield an enormous amount of power and influence in an organization because they are agents of the executives they work for. More importantly, they usually do an incredible amount of work to keep things running smoothly, so anger them at your own (and your career's) peril. And *never* pass up a chance to be nice to an administrative assistant—they are the cornerstone of the Favor Economy.

HOW TO ASK A BUSY EXECUTIVE FOR ANYTHING...VIA EMAIL

Work in any big company long enough, and you'll find yourself in a position where you need to email an executive (or any busy person you don't know) to ask him for something. Perhaps you need something for your product or team, or you are looking to right a wrong. Whatever the case, this is likely the first time you've ever communicated with this person. In this situation, almost everyone makes the same rookie mistake: they ramble, rant, and rave.

Fitz (while working at Apple) bought his mom a lemon of an iMac more than 14 years ago, and on the advice of a coworker sent a "short" email to Steve Jobs.[12] This email served as a rough prototype of how to effectively ask an executive for help:

---

12 Fitz initially penned a mostly incoherent rant to Steve, which would have gotten him absolutely nothing (well, other than a pink slip). His coworker advised that Fitz keep it short and to the point, and to close with a call to action.

Date: Thu, 1 Feb 2001

To: sjobs@apple.com

Subject: Terrible customer experience with our hardware—what can I do?

I would deeply appreciate if you could advise me on what I can do to address this problem. This is embarrassing—both for Apple and for myself.

I purchased an iMac for my mother last Mother's Day—she is the Vice-Principal of a Montessori school in New Orleans and uses an old Macintosh at school. She was very excited to get the iMac, and has even gotten funds for her school to buy iMacs for their lab.

However, the strawberry iMac I bought for her has turned out to be a total lemon.

- In July, it went to sleep and never woke up. She brought it to an Authorized Apple Dealer and they diagnosed the problem as a failed logic board and replaced it.

- She brought it home, plugged it in, it started to boot, then she got a sad mac and the tones of death. She brought it back to the dealer. They diagnosed the problem as a faulty analog board and replaced it.

- In September, I finally convinced her to use the sleep function again (in lieu of shutdown/boot). The iMac wouldn't wake up. Completely unplugging the computer and plugging it back in eventually got it to boot again. We have disabled sleep altogether at this point.

- In December, the monitor started flickering colors from yellow to green to blue. She brought it back to the dealer yesterday, and that's where it is now.

So that's where I am today. My mother thinks I've pulled some sort of sick prank on her, is telling everyone she knows that her iMac is junk, and no one I know that works at Apple knows what to do about it.

Is there anything that I can do to get her a working iMac (short of purchasing another one)?

Respectfully,

-Fitz

Less than 20 hours later Fitz received a call from someone who worked for Steve, and two weeks later his mom had a new (non-lemon-flavored) iMac.

Here's the big secret: when given a chance to help right a wrong, more often than not people in positions of power would *love* to do the right thing—even busy executives (many of them enjoy righting a wrong, and absolutely all of them understand the value of gaining a little extra political capital). Unfortunately, the email inbox of these people looks like a never-ending distributed-denial-of-service attack, and if they encounter an email from someone they've never met before that is 3,000 words of solid text with no paragraph breaks, the odds are good that they're going to read 15 words in, press the Delete key, and then move on to the next email.

If, however, they can fix something by reading an email in 10 seconds and waving a magic wand (i.e., mailing one of their minions to Make It Happen), they'll likely do it. They spend a few seconds delegating and get a big pile of political capital from you in return.

After years of trial and error, we've found that shorter emails are even more likely to get a response.

We call this the "Three Bullets and a Call to Action" technique, and it will drastically increase your chances of getting action—or at the very least, a response—from just about anyone you email out of the blue asking for something,[13] not just an executive.

A good Three Bullets and a Call to Action email contains (at *most*) three bullet points detailing the issue at hand, and one—*and only one*—call to action. That's it, nothing more—you need to write an email that can be easily forwarded along. If you ramble or put four completely different things in the email, you can be certain that they'll pick only one thing to respond to, and it will be the item that you care least about. Or worse, the mental overhead is high enough that your mail will get dropped entirely.

The bullet points should be short sentences (each one should fit on a single line without wrapping), and the call to action should be as short as possible. If you want a reply from *anyone*, make it easier for the person to reply inline, preferably with a one (or two) word answer. Don't ask half a dozen questions in one

---

13 Warning: if you're peanut-butter-hula-hoops crazy, this isn't going to help get you an interview with the President of the United States, a purchase order from Chevy for your laser-powered windshield wiper invention, or lunch with the director of sales for Whole Foods. This technique only applies to realistic requests.

paragraph—limit yourself to a single question per paragraph, or ideally, a single question per email. Lastly, your email should be loaded with HRT: polite, respectful, and devoid of grammar mistakes and spelling errors. If you positively cannot help yourself and simply must include more background or information, put it at the very end of your email (even after your signature), and label it clearly as "More details" or "Background."

In hindsight, we consider Fitz's prototype email to be a bit too wordy—if we were writing it today, it would probably look more like this:

```
Date: Thu, 1 Feb 2001

To: sjobs@apple.com

Subject: Bad customer experience—can you help?

 - I purchased an iMac for my mother, a school administrator. She was
   very excited to get the iMac and has even gotten funds for her
   school to buy more iMacs for their lab.

 - In July, Apple replaced a faulty logic board, and a month later, the
   analog board.

 - In September it stopped sleeping correctly, and in December the
   monitor started to fail. It's currently at the dealer.

My mother is telling everyone she knows that her iMac is junk, and no
one I know that works at Apple knows what to do about it.

Is there anything that I can do to get her a working iMac?

Respectfully,

-Fitz
```

This rewritten email eliminates a lot of the editorial color, but is now readable by a busy executive in 10 seconds.

In the course of our careers, we've used all of these techniques over and over again to get things done. But sometimes all the tips and tricks in the world aren't enough to fix a job.

Plan B: Get Out

In all the years that we've spoken about getting things done inside bad organizations and working with bad people, we always get people who come up to us after our talks and, exasperated, tell us they've tried *everything* and just can't make any improvements or get anything done, so what can they do? The unfortunate answer here is a simple one: there's probably nothing else you *can* do. Don't be a victim. Get the heck out of there.

If you can't change the system, there's no point in continuing to put energy into changing it. Instead, put energy into leaving it: update your résumé, and start asking your close friends if they know of any openings for you at other companies. Train yourself in new things. One of the great things about being a knowledge worker in this day and age is that good ones are in high demand, and that gives you the ability to control your own future.

Once you realize you have this control, it's incredibly liberating. If you poke around and discover that you have other job options available to you, you may discover that you suddenly get a lot more things done at your work (under a lot less stress) because it's not the end of the world if your current employer fires you! We found this blog post[14] from Chade-Meng Tan, Google's longtime "Jolly Good Fellow," incredibly inspiring and it has greatly influenced how we do our own jobs:

Do the right thing, wait to get fired

New Google employees (we call "Nooglers") often ask me what makes me effective at what I do. I tell them only half-jokingly that it's very simple: I do the Right Thing for Google and the world, and then I sit back and wait to get fired. If I don't get fired, I've done the Right Thing for everyone. If I do get fired, this is the wrong employer to work for in the first place. So, either way, I win. That is my career strategy.

If you're prepared and know your options, you're the most liberated person in the world. Don't be afraid to get out. We've been giving this advice after our talks for over five years now, and are happy to report that several people have emailed us to let us know that they heeded our advice and are now doing jobs that they love. And these emails are some of the best we've ever gotten—here's one of our favorites:

```
Date: Thu, 1 Dec 2011
Subject: Thank you note
From: Alex Mrvaljevich
To: Brian Fitzpatrick

Hello Brian!

You probably don't remember me, but you gave me the best two pieces of
career advice i have ever gotten, and changed my life.

I attended your tech talk @ Google IO 2010 and approached you after the
talk to ask about advice on my current work situation. Quite simply you
told me to "get the hell out" so i sent you my CV as Project Manager; After
this you let me know that google RARELY hires non-technical project
```

---

14 *http://bit.ly/do_right_thing*

```
managers.

Because of that i had to think long and hard about my career: Whatever
Google's policy is, majority of companies follow suit.

Changing career tracks was my only option, my closest bet was Product
Management. Studied my ass off and "got the hell out" not only of the
company I was in, but also of the country (There aren't a lot of
Product Management jobs in Venezuela), it ended up being the best move
in my life...

Now because of that move I just landed an amazing job as Product Lead in
Japan, and am moving to Kobe in February.

I promised myself if things ever turned around because of that piece of
advice I would send you a thank you note, so here it is:

Thank you.

Alex
```

All Is Not Lost

All this talk about quitting or waiting to get fired doesn't mean that if you're unhappy in your job you should dust off your résumé and hit the streets. On the contrary, your first objective should be to make the changes necessary to be happy and accomplish your goals at your job, and this chapter has given you a lot of the tools you'll need to do that. If you don't put the effort into understanding how to navigate your organization, you're leaving a huge part of your destiny to chance.

6

Users Are People, Too

We've explored a long list of ingredients that are critical to successful product development.

Start with a small group of smart, creative people. Fertilize the team with a strong culture of humility, trust, and respect. Lead them as a servant, empowering them to collaborate and make good decisions. Give them water, sunlight, direction, and intrinsic motivation as needed. Protect them from negative influences—destructive behaviors (or environments) that threaten the culture and the ability to make progress. Bake at 72°F for six months, and you've got some great software. All done, right?

A lot of programmers stop there. They write software for themselves, are pleased with the end result, and then declare victory.

Unfortunately, that's not how the real world works. "Good software" is an overly narrow definition of success. If you're trying to pay the bills (or simply boost your résumé) you also need a lot of other people to use your software and be happy with it. The software development process doesn't end with throwing a product over a wall; it never ends, in fact. People use your product and you need to react to them, improving it over time. If you don't learn how to master this feedback loop your creation will die.

We'll examine three general phases of user engagement in this chapter. First you need to get users to notice your work—are they even aware that it exists? How do they perceive it before they walk in the door? Then you'll need to think about what people experience when they start using it. Does it meet their expectations? Is it usable? Does it empower them to do great things? Finally, we'll look at how to interact productively with them once they're firmly engaged with your creation. All of these interactions are part of the cyclical nature of product development.

The bottom line is this: collaboration isn't just about working with your team; to make great things, you need to actively collaborate with your *users* too.

If you're not on top of these things, all you'll have is a piece of shiny software with no users. If that's the case, maybe it's time to question your career choice!

Managing Public Perception

When you hear the term *marketing*, what's the first thing that comes to mind?

If you're like most folks, the word probably conjures up the image of a dishonest salesperson, all fake smile and greased-back hair: somebody who's all about building an image for a client or product. If your product is the raw "meat" to be sold, the marketing person's job is to add the magic "sizzle" to the steak so that more people flock to it.

Why does this idea bug us so much? Why do we shudder at the thought of the marketing person?

Because, as programmers, the marketer represents the antithesis of engineering culture. We're obsessed with truth. Either the code compiles or it doesn't; the software has a feature or it doesn't; it solves a problem or it doesn't. We don't "spin" our descriptions of the world; we state the facts and then work to change them. We look at the marketing guy and all we see are lies, and we don't like being lied to. We want order, predictability, and accurate statements when it comes to making decisions.

Because we perceive marketing as something that distorts the truth, it violates the maker's instinctive desire for meritocracy. We believe the best product should always win. And by "best" we mean the product that *objectively* is of the highest quality and most effective, not the one with the slickest TV advertisements. Over and over we're disappointed when we see superior technologies lose out: many believe that Betamax was superior to VHS, that Laserdisc was better than DVD, or that Lisp is still the best programming language (we just need to get the word out!). Even in the world of version control tools, Subversion has taken over the corporate world despite the technical superiority of newer systems like Git.

What's worse is we perceive marketing folks as overpromising to customers, which in turn makes engineers look like they're always underdelivering. It makes steam pour from our ears.

We're here to give you both bad news and good news.

The bad news is that no, you cannot ignore marketing. It actually matters and you have to deal with it. The good news is that it's possible to actively cooperate with marketing. It doesn't need to be a sleazy affair when you do it right. In fact, it can be an incredibly powerful tool to success!

Programmers tend to have an overdeveloped sense of logic, but most humans are driven equally by logic *and* emotion. The marketing folks are masters of emotional manipulation, and that's why they're so effective: they mix the facts with feelings to get attention. If you want to get new people to use your software, you *have to care* about their emotional perception of your software. You cannot change the way people make decisions.

Apple Inc. is the undisputed master of making technology appeal to the emotions of nontechnical people. Firmly dating ourselves in the year 2015, we ask: is an iPhone objectively superior to an Android phone? Featurewise they're almost identical. But if a nontechnical user believes an iPhone is magical, it really *is* magical, at least to that user. Perception is reality. Or as we've said earlier, "Perception is nine-tenths of the law."

It's tempting to think that the only way to win is not to play, but this is a game you're not allowed to ignore. You need at least a minimal marketing strategy to even get your software in the ring, and if you're smart about it then you'll discover that marketing can be a serious force multiplier for great engineering. Here are some basic things you can do to take control, and they're all based on HRT.

PAY ATTENTION TO FIRST IMPRESSIONS

If you're hungry and searching for a restaurant, how the restaurant appears from the street really matters. If it seems disgusting or uninviting you simply aren't going in. If it's warm and friendly and the host is kind, you'll be willing to give it a fair chance. Don't underestimate the emotional impact of a well-designed first experience with your product—if you've ever unboxed an iPad or a Nest thermostat, you know exactly what we mean here.

What is your product like to a newbie? Is it welcoming and does it encourage exploration? Conversely, for an expert who sits down to an initial session with your software, does it appear familiar and sensible? At first glance, does your app scream instant productivity, or steep learning curve and countless tears? More specifically, what does a user experience in the first 30 seconds after launching your software? Don't just give an intellectual answer ("she sees a menu of choices, with a login box") but give an emotional answer too. How does a new user *feel* after a minute? Empowered or just confused? What can you do to improve that feeling? Step back a level and look at your product's website. Does it seem professional and inviting, like a good storefront? You need to take these things seriously for your software to be taken seriously.

UNDERPROMISE AND OVERDELIVER

Don't let your marketing people preempt you here. If users ask about upcoming features or release timelines, take the opportunity to give overly conservative estimates. If you let marketers spread rumors, you'll end up with a *Duke Nukem Forever* situation—software that's teased for shipping *15 years* late. But if your own (more accurate) message gets out first, your users will always be thrilled. Google is great at this; it has a deliberate policy of *not* preannouncing features for any product. When new features roll out they're often a delightful surprise. It also prevents internal death marches to meet unrealistic advertised launch dates. The software is released when it's actually ready and usable.

WORK WITH INDUSTRY ANALYSTS RESPECTFULLY

A lot of programmers hate the media industry—it's just marketing in another guise. When a trade magazine or research firm comes knocking on the door, a lot of companies will drop everything and kowtow to their requests. They realize that a good (or bad) review can make or break a product's perception. Engineers tend to resent this sort of power and deference, though.

For example, there was a time when members of the Apache Software Foundation (ASF) had problems interacting with analysts. An analyst would ask the ASF for industry-standard white papers describing their Apache HTTPD server, and the typical snarky response might be, "Go read the documentation on the website, like everyone else." While this satisfied the open source developers' deep commitment to meritocracy, overall it was counterproductive to public perception—particularly among corporate users. Eventually the ASF "PR person" worked to reeducate a number of community members about this attitude and deal more productively with analysts. Passive-aggressively fighting the system—no matter how irritating it is—just doesn't make sense. It's no different from telling the restaurant reviewer to get back at the end of the line. Should the reviewer get preferential treatment? Probably not. But is it worth sticking it to him as a matter of principle? *Definitely* not. You're only hurting yourself in the process. Choose your battles carefully.

How Usable Is Your Software?

Here's a hard truth: unless you're developing software tools, engineers are not the audience of your software. The corollary is that you, as an engineer, are a terrible evaluator of your software's usability. An interface that seems totally reasonable to you may very likely make your nontechie neighbor pull out her hair in frustration.

If we assume that "successful software" means "lots of people use and love your software," you need to pay deep attention to your users. Google has a famous motto:

Focus on the user, and all else will follow.

It sounds fairly campy, but over our careers we've watched this maxim play out over and over across multiple projects. We've witnessed projects succeed and fail based on this truth.

One of Google's big breakthroughs was to begin measuring the effectiveness of search ads. If users click on a particular ad, it must be useful to them; if it never gets clicks, it must be annoying or useless. Bad ads get removed from the system and feedback is given to the advertiser to improve its ads. At first this seems counterproductive for the short term: Google is actively rejecting revenue sources. But by making the *searcher* (rather than the advertiser) the focus of attention, it dramatically increases the usefulness (and usage) of Google's search advertising system over the long term.

Let's talk about some important ways you can focus directly on your users.

CHOOSE YOUR AUDIENCE

First things first: imagine your users fall across a spectrum of technical competence.

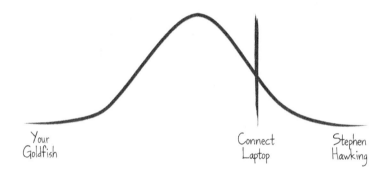

If you were to draw a vertical line showing *which set of users* is best suited to your product, where would you put it? A vertical line through the center of the bell curve means that about half of all computer users would be happy using your product (i.e., those to the right of the line).

As an example, let's take the problem of wanting to display Internet content on your large TV screen. How has the "usability" of competing solutions widened potential audiences? Initially people had to plug their laptop computers directly into their televisions. This involved understanding analog versus digital inputs and having the right sort of audio and video cables.

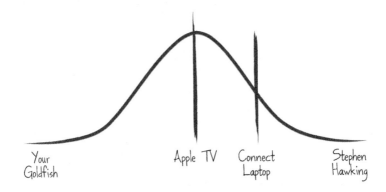

Apple then came out with an Apple TV product—a small computer-like appliance that you left permanently plugged into your TV. It could be controlled from a computer or smartphone, and you could stream either your private media or live Internet content. This solved the problem for a much larger (and less technical) audience: it came with the proper cables, and you plugged it in once and left it there.

Google then one-upped things by coming out with the Chromecast, a small stick that plugs directly into a TV's HDMI port. It was even easier to install and allowed people to "cast" their screen from a wider array of both Apple *and* non-Apple devices. At the time of writing, we're now seeing new TVs being shipped with built-in WiFi and Internet streaming. It's likely that Ben's kids will never remember a time when TVs didn't have Netflix built in!

The point here is that good product development aims to move the vertical line to the *left* as much as possible. In general, the more users you have, the more successful you are (and the more money your company makes!). The moral here is that when you're considering your users, think hard about who your audience is. Is your work usable by the biggest group possible? This is why simple and thoughtful user interfaces matter so much—as well as things like polished documentation and accessible tutorials.

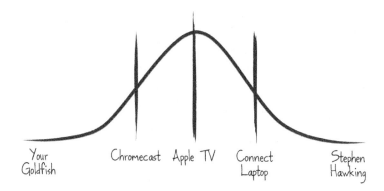

CONSIDER BARRIER TO ENTRY

Now think about the first-time users of your software. How hard is it to get going for the first time? If your users can't easily try it out, you won't have any. A first-time user usually isn't thinking about whether your software is more or less powerful than a competitor's; she just wants to get something done. Quickly.

To illustrate, take a look at popular scripting languages. A majority of programmers will espouse that Perl or Python is a "better" language than PHP. They'll claim that Perl/Python/Ruby programs are easier to read and maintain over the long run, have more mature libraries, and are inherently safer and more secure when exposed to the open Web. Yet PHP is far more popular—at least for web development. Why? Because any high school student can just pick it up through osmosis by copying his buddy's website. There's no need to read books, do extensive tutorials, or learn serious programming patterns. It's conducive to tinkering: just start hacking on your site and figure out different PHP tricks from your peers.

Another example can be found in text editors. Should programmers use Emacs or vi? Does it matter? Not really, but why would a person choose one over the other? Here's a true anecdote: when Ben first started learning Unix (during an internship in 1990) he was looking for a text editor to launch. He opened an existing file by launching vi for the first time, and was utterly frustrated within 20 seconds—he could move around within the file, but couldn't type anything! Of course, vi users know that one has to enter "edit" mode to change the file, but it was still a horrible first experience for a newbie. When Ben launched Emacs instead, he could immediately begin editing a file just like he would do on his familiar home word processor. Because the initial behavior of Emacs was identical to his previous experiences, Ben decided to become an Emacs user within his first minute. It's a silly reason to choose one product over another, but this sort of thing happens all the time! That first minute with a product is *critical*.[1]

Of course, there are other ways to destroy the first impression. The first time your software runs, don't present the user with a giant form to fill out or a giant panel of mandatory preferences to set. Forcing the user to create some sort of new account is pretty off-putting as well; it implies long-term commitment before the user has even done anything. Another personal pet peeve is a website instantly blasting a visitor with a modal "Subscribe to us!" dialog box within the first two seconds. All these things send the user screaming in the other direction.

A great example of a nearly invisible barrier to entry is the TripIt web service, which is designed to manage travel itineraries. To start using the service simply forward your existing travel-confirmation emails (airplane, hotel, rental car, etc.) to *plans@tripit.com*. Poof, you're now using TripIt. The service creates a temporary account for you, parses your emails, creates a gorgeous itinerary page, and then sends an email to tell you it's ready. It's like a personal assistant instantly showing up, and all you did was forward a few messages! With almost no effort on your part, you've been sucked in and are browsing the website as an involved user. At this point, you're willing to create a real service account.

If you're skeptical about your own product's barrier to entry, try doing some simple tests. Give your software to ordinary humans—both technical and nontechnical—and observe their first minute or two. You may be surprised at what you discover.

---

1 Of course *overall* Emacs is probably just as complex to learn as vi—but we're talking about first impressions rather than logic.

MEASURE USAGE, NOT USERS

In pondering the size of your user base and whether it's easy to get started, you should also consider how you measure usage. Notice that we said "usage," not "number of installs"—you want a high number of users who *use* your product, not a high number of times people *download* your product. You'll often hear someone say, "Hey, my product has had 3 million downloads—that's 3 million happy users!" Wait; back up. How many of those 3 million users are *actually using* your software? That's what we mean by "usage."

As an extreme example, how many machines is the Unix archive utility "ar" installed on? Answer: just about every Unix-based OS out there, including all versions of Linux, Mac OS X, BSD, and so on. And how many people use that program? How many even know what it is? Here we have a piece of software with millions of installs but near-zero usage.

Usage is something that many companies (including Google) spend a lot of time measuring. Common metrics include "7-day actives" and "30-day actives"— that is, how many users have used the software in the past week or month. These are the important numbers that actually tell you how well your software is doing. Ignore the download counts. Figure out a way to measure ongoing activity instead. For example, if your product is a website or web app, try a product like Google Analytics; it not only gives you these metrics, but also gives you insight into where your users came from, how long they stayed, and so on. These are incredibly useful indicators of product uptake.

Design Matters

Before the Internet came into prominence, the biggest challenge to getting any product to market was one of distribution. Few companies had the wherewithal to write a product *and* get it into thousands of stores across the world, so when a company put a product out there, they would then market the hell out of it. This typically resulted in one or two "winners" in each software category (e.g., Microsoft Word versus WordPerfect, Excel vs. Lotus 1-2-3, etc.). The primary criteria you used when choosing a product were features and cost, no matter how ugly or unintuitive the software was.

That, however, has changed.

The Internet is a global distribution network where it costs almost nothing to find and download software. And social media makes it easy for people to share their feelings about various products across the globe in seconds. The result of these two massive changes (and a host of other, smaller factors) means that consumers today have a choice of what product to use. In this highly competitive environment, it's no longer enough to just get a product out there with the necessary features—your product needs to be beautiful and easy to use. These days, no amount of marketing will rescue a crappy product, but a well-designed product that delights the people that use it will turn these same people into evangelists that market the product *for* you.

So good design is key, but a big part of good design is putting the user first, hiding complexity, making your product fast, and, most importantly, not being all things to all people.

PUT THE USER FIRST

When we say to "put the user first," we're suggesting that you and your team should take on whatever hard product work you can to make using your product easier for your users. This may mean some hard engineering work, but more frequently it means making hard design decisions instead of letting your users make these decisions every time they use your product. We refer to this as *product laziness*. Some would argue that laziness is a virtue for engineers because it leads to efficient automation of work. On the other hand, it can be easy to create something that results in great pain for users. Making software easy for users is one of the greatest challenges in product development.

A classic example of this kind of laziness is to present too many options to your users. People love to make fun of the late-1990s generation of Microsoft

Office products: button bars! They make every possible menu item instantly available...for great convenience! User interface designers love to make fun of this idea, especially when taken to an extreme:

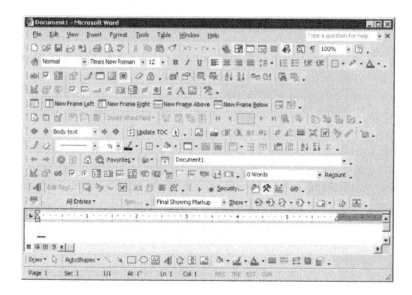

Having too many options is overwhelming. It's intimidating and off-putting. There have even been books written about how too many choices create anxiety and misery.[2] You even need to be careful within your software's Preferences dialog. (Did you know that Eudora, a popular email client, had 30 different panels of preference values?) And if you're making someone fill out a form, be lenient in what you accept: deal with extra whitespace, punctuation, or dashes. Don't make the user do the parsing! It's about respecting the user's time. It's really obvious (and infuriating) when a programmer *could* have made something friendly and easy for the end user but didn't bother.

SPEED MATTERS

Most programmers vastly underestimate the importance of *application speed* (or *latency,* which sounds more scientific). Its effects are both fundamental and profound.

---

2 See Barry Schwartz's *The Paradox of Choice: Why More Is Less* (Ecco).

First, latency is another type of "barrier to entry." We've become spoiled about web page speed. When told to check out a new website, if it doesn't load within three or four seconds, people often abort and lose interest. There's simply no excuse here. The web browser makes it easy to walk away and redirect our attention to 12 other places. We have better things to do than wait for a page to load.

Second, when a program responds quickly, it has a deep subliminal effect on users. They start using it more and more because it feels frictionless. It becomes an unconscious extension of their abilities. On the other hand, a slow application becomes increasingly frustrating over time. Users start using the software less and less, often without even realizing it.

After a product launches, it's exciting to see usage grow over time. But after a while the usage often hits a limit—it just sort of flatlines. This is the point where the marketing folks often step in and scream about needing more features, prettier colors, nicer fonts, or more animations that "pop." Sometimes, however, the *actual* reason for the stall is latency. The program has become laggy and frustrating. As the next graph shows, user engagement decreases as latency increases.

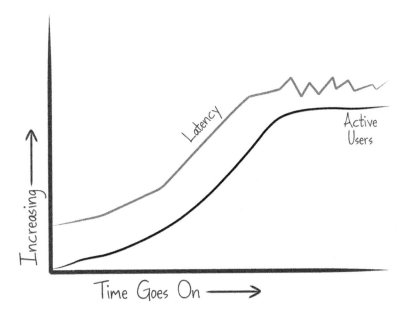

A true story from Google: an engineering team one day released some dramatic latency improvements to Google Maps. There was no announcement, no blog post; the launch was completely secret and silent. Yet the activity graph showed a huge (and permanent) jump in usage within the first couple of days. There's some powerful psychology going on there!

Even small improvements in latency matter when you're serving a web-based application. Suppose it takes 750 milliseconds for your main application screen to load. That seems fast enough, right? Not too frustrating for any given user. But if you could slash your load times to 250 milliseconds, that extra half of a second makes a huge difference in aggregate. If you have a million users each doing 20 requests per day, that amounts to *116 years* of saved user time—stop killing your users! Improving latency is one of the best ways to increase usage and make your users happy. As Google's founders like to say, "Speed is a feature."

DON'T TRY TO BE ALL THINGS

Is your software trying to accomplish too much? This sounds like a silly question at first, but some of the worst software out there is bad because it's overly ambitious. It tries to be absolutely everything to everyone. Some of the best software succeeds because it defines the problem narrowly and solves it well. Instead of solving every problem badly, it solves really common problems for *most* users and does it really well.

We often joke about certain gadgets we see in magazine ads: hey, look, it's a camping lantern, with a built-in weather radio!...and, uh, also a built-in TV, and um, stopwatch, and alarm clock, and...eh? It's a confusing mess. Instead, think of your software as a simple toaster oven. Does it cook everything? Absolutely not. But it cooks *a lot* of really common food and is useful to almost everyone who encounters it without being overwhelming. Be the toaster oven. Less is more.

HIDE COMPLEXITY

"But my software is complex," you may think, "and it's solving a complex problem. So why should I try to hide that?" That's a reasonable concern, but it's also one of the central challenges of good product design. An elegant design makes easy things easy and hard things possible. Even when doing complex things your software should *feel* seamless and easy. (Again, we're focusing on the user's emotions.)

This is what we like to call "hiding the complexity." You take a complex problem and break it up, cover it, or do something to make the software seem simple anyway.

Look at Apple again. Apple's product design is legendary, and one of the cleverest things it did was to creatively tackle the problem of managing MP3 music collections. Before iPods came along, there were a handful of awkward gizmos that tried to manage music right on the portable device. Apple's genius was to realize that MP3 management was too difficult a problem to solve on a tiny screen, so it *moved* the solution to a big computer. iTunes was the answer. You use your computer (with big screen, keyboard, and mouse) to manage your music collection, and then use the iPod *only* for playback. The iPod can then be simple and elegant, and organizing your music is no longer frustrating.

Google Search is another well-known example of hiding complexity. Google's interface (and barrier to entry) is almost nonexistent: it's just a magic box to type in. Yet behind that box, there are thousands of machines across the planet responding in parallel and doing a search after *every keystroke* you type. By the time you hit Enter, the search results have already rendered on your screen. The amount of technology behind that text box is jaw-dropping, and yet the complexity of the problem is hidden from the user. It behaves like Magic.[3] This is a great goal for a creative team to pursue since it's essentially the epitome of product usability.

Finally, we should mention a caveat about complexity. While masking complexity is laudable, it is *not* a goal to seal the software so tight that it ends up handcuffing all your users. Hiding complexity almost always involves creating clever abstractions, and as a programmer you need to assume that the abstractions will eventually "leak." When a web browser prints a 404 error, that's a leaked abstraction; the illusion is cracked. Don't panic, though—it's better to assume that abstractions are leaky and simply embrace them by providing deliberate ways to lift the curtain. A great way to do this is to provide APIs to other programmers. Or for really advanced users, create an "expert mode" that provides more options and choices for those who want to bypass the abstractions.

Not only is it important to keep the interface flexible and circumventable, but the user's data needs to be accessible as well. Fitz put a great deal of passion into making sure Google products offer "data liberation"—that it's trivial for a user to export his data from an application and walk away. Software shouldn't lock users in, no matter how elegant the interface is. Allowing users to open the hood and do whatever they want with their data forces you to compete honestly: people use your software because they *want* to, not because they're trapped. It's about engendering trust, which (as we'll mention) is your most sacred resource.

---

3 See Arthur C. Clarke's Third Law (*http://bit.ly/clarkes_3rd_law*).

Managing Your Relationship with Users

OK, so your product is appealing on first sight. It's easy to get started. And once people begin, it's really pleasant. What happens months down the line? How do you interact with people who use your product every day, for years at a time?

Believe it or not, many users *want* to have a relationship with your company or team. Happy users want to know what's going on with your software's evolution; angry users want a place to complain. One of the biggest mistakes programmers make is to toss software over a wall and then stop listening to feedback.

Like *marketing*, the term *customer service* also typically has a negative connotation. A career in "customer service" often conjures up an image of a barista working at a coffee shop or a room full of robotic people answering support calls. But in reality, customer service isn't a nasty, soul-draining task; nor is it something that other people (with lesser job descriptions) do. It's a philosophy to live by—a way of thinking about your ongoing connection to users. It's something you need to do proactively as a creative team, not as a mere reaction to external complaints.

Engineers often dread direct interactions with users. "Users are clueless," they think. "They're annoying and impossible to talk to." And while nobody's requiring you to shower every user with love, the simple fact is that *users want to be heard.* Even if they make inane suggestions or clueless complaints, the most important thing you can possibly do is *acknowledge* them. The more you allow them to participate in the discussion and development process, the more loyal and happy they'll be. You don't have to agree with them, but you still need to listen. This is the "Respect" in HRT! Companies are rapidly learning this in the age of social media—just reaching out to someone as a human and not as a giant, faceless corporation is often enough to alleviate that person's concerns. People love it when corporations openly display HRT.

We like to illustrate the importance of managing users over time by drawing another simple (slightly unscientific) graph. As time goes on, your software gains more and more users. Of course, as you "improve" the product, it also gains more and more complexity:

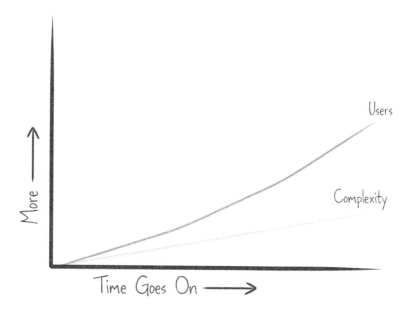

The problem here is that as the number of users increases, their average level of technical ability *decreases*, because you're covering more and more of the general population. Pair this up with ever-increasing complexity and you've got a serious issue with users' despair:

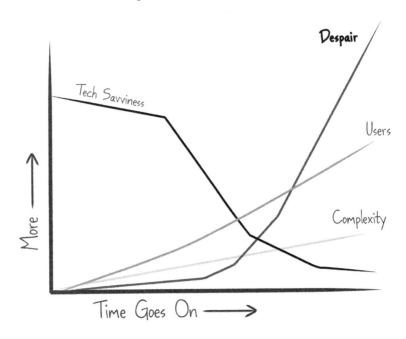

More despair means more complaints, angrier users, and an ever-increasing need for open communication with the software developers!

What can you do to avoid this trend?

To begin, don't be in denial about the problem. Many corporations instinctively do everything they can to put up walls of bureaucracy between programmers and users. They create voicemail trees to navigate through or file complaints as "help tickets" that are tracked by layers of people who aren't actually writing the software. Messages are relayed only indirectly through these layers, as though direct contact with the dangerous rabble might endanger developers (or pointlessly distract them). This is how users end up feeling ignored and disempowered and how developers end up completely disconnected.

A much better mode of interaction is to directly acknowledge users. Give them a public bug tracker to complain in and respond to them directly. Create an email list for them to help one another. Interact directly with users in social media. If your product can be open source, that's a huge help as well. The more "human" you appear to users, the more they trust in the product, and despair begins to lessen. Be on the lookout for people using your products in unexpected (and awesome) ways. Only through true dialogue can you discover what they're really doing with your software, possibly something clever or thrilling.

RESPECT USERS' INTELLIGENCE

Give users respect by default. A common misconception that powers our fear of direct user interaction is the myth that users are stupid. They're not writing the software, after all, so they're just "clueless users," right? When you finally have an opportunity to interact with them, the most important thing to remember is to avoid condescension. Being a savvy computer user is *not* a fair measure of general intelligence. A lot of brilliant people out there use computers as a tool and nothing more. They're not interested in debugging or following scientific methods to diagnose a problem. Remember that most of us have no idea how to take apart and fix our cars; assuming your users are stupid is akin to an auto mechanic thinking *you* are stupid because you don't know how to rebuild a transmission, nor even care how to diagnose a transmission problem. The car is a black box—you just want to drive. For most people, the computer (and your software) is a black box, too. Users don't want to participate in the analysis process; they just want to get some work done. It has nothing to do with intelligence!

BE PATIENT

The corollary, then, is to learn great patience. Most users simply don't have the vocabulary to express their problems succinctly. It takes years of practice to learn to understand what they're saying: just ask anyone who has tried to provide computer tech support to his parents over the phone (which is probably most of you reading this book!). Half of the discussion comprises just trying to agree on the same vocabulary. Many people don't know what a web browser is, thinking it's just part of their computer. They describe applications as actions, or talk about screen icons as mysterious workflow names. The thing is, even the most intelligent folks have a knack for creating their own logical universe (and vocabulary) that explains how computers behave. They begin to diagnose problems in terms of imaginary taxonomies and rules that exist only in their minds.

Parent: "I think my computer is slow because the disk is full."

You: "How do you know the disk is full? Did you check?"

Parent: "Yeah, well, the screen is totally covered with icons, so there's probably no more room for my email to download. Maybe I can delete some cookies to make more space, huh? That seemed to work last time."

You: [Facepalm]

The critical listening skill here is to learn to understand what people *mean*, not necessarily to try to interpret what they literally *say*. It requires not just some language translation, but some emotional intelligence as well. And mind reading.

Fitz has a great story about his grandmother in which she asked him (over the phone), "Brian, is that old computer of grandpa's worth anything at all?" Fitz said no, that it was just a very old Mac Classic without an Internet connection— probably best to safely recycle it. Her response: "OK, well, I only turn it on when I need to sharpen a pencil."

After a prolonged moment of utter confusion, Fitz decided he needed to start questioning her so that he could figure out just what she meant!

It turns out that both the Mac and grandma's electric pencil sharpener were plugged into a power strip. Once a week grandma would come into the room with her pencils and turn on the power strip. The Mac would beep and begin to boot. Grandma would sharpen her pencils and then cut the strip's power when she left the room, abruptly killing the Mac before it could even finish booting.[4] This is a great example of a nontechnical person attempting to explain a situation using limited vocabulary and whatever model has sprung up around her relationship to the computer.

---

4 In case you're concerned, the Mac has since been put out of its misery.

A lot of people also have magical preconceptions of Google's search service. Many people think it's just part of their computer. In 2005, we used to get puzzled looks from people when we told them we were engineers at Google: "Oh! I didn't know anyone worked there?!" On the flip side, a friend of Fitz's grandmother once got upset when she heard the entire company was going to go on an off-site ski trip. (This was back when the company was still small.) "That's terrible! How can they all go skiing?" she asked. "Who's going to do all my searches for me?" Clearly, Google was being negligent, not leaving enough switchboard operators to keep the traffic running.

CREATE TRUST AND DELIGHT

There are two more watchwords that should become the cornerstones of the way you interact with users: *trust* and *delight*.

Trust is a tricky term. We've already talked about trust in the context of HRT—about whether and how you exhibit trust toward your coworkers. In this case we're talking about garnering trust from users. When a user trusts your team (or your company) it's mainly an emotional state: very few people would ever say, "I trust product X because of this long list of facts that prove that my relationship with it carries zero risk." They trust you because the cumulative set of interactions they've had with you add up to an overall *emotionally* positive state.

Think about your friends and family for a moment. How many of them have an auto mechanic they really trust? These days the answer is nearly zero. Almost nobody trusts auto mechanics, because we've been badgered by years of what is called "mailboxing": when you come in for one scheduled service (like an oil change), but a bunch of other unexpected maintenance services are piled on, much like junk mail stuffed into your mailbox. Nobody believes mechanics anymore because they've been instructed to maximize profit at every opportunity. Remember, *there is no such thing as a temporary lapse of integrity.*

This is a great example of how the long-term relationship can be easily sacrificed for short-term gain. Screw your customers just a teeny bit every now and then, and eventually they view the relationship through a veil of aggregated disdain. On the other hand, every time your team does something helpful or useful, or is responsive, a bit of trust is added to an imaginary bank account in their minds. When a baker adds a surprise 13th donut to your dozen ("lagniappe," as they call it in New Orleans), this brings a smile to your face. Over years of dealings the trust account grows and grows until the mention of your product brings a warm, fuzzy feeling.

Trust can be dangerous, however, because it can be blown all at once—just like a bank account can be drained with a single stupid, impulsive purchase. If your company does something that shows a total lack of respect for users (even if by accident), the trust bank is emptied overnight.

A good example of this is the way Netflix temporarily messed up its relationship with users in late 2011. Netflix is both a service for streaming movies over the Internet and also a way for renting DVDs by postal mail. Over the period of a decade it became increasingly popular: it was easy, convenient, and novel. The price was cheap. By early 2011 it had more than 23 million subscribers.

At some point the business folks realized their DVD and streaming services were really separate businesses with separate profit models, management needs, and so on. So they decided to start charging for these businesses separately, raising their monthly fees 60% for some users. Customers were furious. Then Netflix announced that it would be splitting into two separate companies for greater clarity and convenience; to users this simply read as "now you have the annoyance of two bills to pay instead of one." Realizing they had a PR disaster on their hands, they then *unannounced* the splitting of the company, but by that time it was too late. The damage had been done. Despite a history of continuous growth they lost 800,000 subscribers in the span of three months. They managed to blow most of a decade's worth of trust with just a couple of small moves that seemed like simple and necessary business decisions, but had little regard for existing relationships. (Luckily, they managed to totally rebuild their bank of trust over the next few years by paying careful attention to service and content; they came back even stronger!)

Trust is your *most sacred resource.* Watch it carefully. Measure the size of the bank account. Before every move, think about how it will affect the bank account. Focus on your long-term image, not short-term conveniences.

Like trust, *delight* is another feeling that can vastly improve your relationship with users. It's a way of increasing that warm, fuzzy feeling, and making your team seem more human.

You have to start by not taking yourself too seriously. Google has a tradition of making outlandish product announcements on April Fools Day; for example, one year, every video on the front page of YouTube caused a "rickroll." Or take a look at *www.woot.com.* It's a daily deal site, but the advertising copy is full of self-deprecating and quirky humor.

Try to surprise your users with amazing, wonderful bits of happiness. (That's the definition of delight, isn't it?) Despite Google being a powerhouse of hard computer science, nothing excites its users more than the occasional "doodle" that illustrates a holiday or anniversary. It's just a tiny bit of artwork injected into people's day and yet it inspires endless letters of feedback and office water-cooler discussions.

Of course, a bit of horror can inspire users as well, as long as it's done humorously. A company trying to start a social network once wanted to encourage new users to upload pictures of themselves; eventually the company decided to start showing a picture of snarling Dick Cheney for every user who hadn't done so—and the photo uploads suddenly started pouring in!

Adding bits of delight and humor—tactfully—goes a long way toward showing that you're actually paying attention to users and care about your relationship with them.

Remember the Users

We've covered a slew of ideas in this chapter, but in the end, it all boils down to three simple concepts that you can stick in your pocket:

Marketing
> Be aware of how people perceive your software; it determines whether they even try it out.

Product design
> If your software isn't easy to try, fast, friendly, and accessible, users will walk away.

Customer service
> Proactive engagement with long-term users affects your software's evolution and user retention.

Our day jobs as programmers are so full of distractions—code reviews, design reviews, fighting with our tools, putting out production-related fires, triaging bugs—that it's easy to forget the *reason* we're writing software at all. It's not for you, or your team, or your company. It's to make life easier for users. It's critical to pay attention to what they're thinking and saying about your product and how they're experiencing it over the long run. Your users are the lifeblood of your software's success. You reap what you sow.

Epilogue

By now it should be pretty clear that most of the advice in our book isn't necessarily specific to product development.

Our stories are essentially about the art of maintaining a healthy, functional community—*any* community. You could take our anecdotes, remove the parts specific to product development, and substitute any other sort of activity. We could be talking about a neighborhood club, a church group, a fraternity, or a construction team; the same social problems exist and the same solutions are applicable. Humans are unpredictable and tricky to deal with no matter what the context. Product development has the same community-health issues as any other group endeavor.

So, while you're out there busily incorporating HRT into your daily work life, keep in mind that it applies to the rest of your life as well.

Who knows? It's possible that our real calling may be in writing church sermons. But for now we'll stick to writing software and getting the most out of collaboration. And now you have the power to do that, too.

A Final Thought

We've covered an awful lot of topics in this book. After you close the cover it may be hard to figure out which parts to embrace in your daily life. After all, what's the point of reading a book like this if it doesn't result in some changes in the way you work? What happens now?

Let's keep things simple. If you remember anything at all about our stories, remember HRT: humility, respect, and trust.

As we explained in the first chapter, these three core traits are the things that need to underlie every social action you make and every relationship you cultivate. And if you look carefully you'll find that nearly every social problem stems from a *lack* of one of these traits.

Remember that HRT applies to all your different "spheres" of influence. It applies to you before anything else: these traits affect every individual communication you make. It applies to your team: a culture based on humility, respect, and trust will spend the most time coding and the least time infighting. It applies to the way people lead teams: skilled leaders serve their teams and not the other way around. HRT also applies to the way you interoperate with and survive temporary collaborators outside your team, whether they are nice folks, jerks, or a dysfunctional bureaucracy. And finally, these principles apply directly to the way you interact with the most important group of all—the users of your product.

If you keep HRT at the forefront of the way you work, you'll have greater impact with considerably less effort. We think it's the best way to end up spending the most amount of time doing what you love (shipping product) and the least amount of time dealing with social conflicts, bureaucracy, and other human drama.

Further Reading

We created this book based on our experiences writing software with numerous teams and people, but we've also read many books and articles that have helped us formulate the thoughts that we laid out on these pages. Here are a few of the books and articles that influenced us along the way:

- *Peopleware: Productive Projects and Teams*, 2nd Edition, by Tom DeMarco (Dorset House)

- *Drive: The Surprising Truth About What Motivates Us* by Daniel H. Pink (Riverhead)

- "You and Your Research" (*http://bit.ly/hamming_paper*) by Richard Hamming

- *Predictably Irrational: The Hidden Forces That Shape Our Decisions* by Dan Ariely (HarperCollins)

- *The Mythical Man-Month: Essays on Software Engineering*, 2nd Edition, by Frederick P. Brooks (Addison-Wesley Professional)

- *Startup Engineering Management* by Piaw Na (self-published)

- *Rework* (*http://37signals.com/rework*) by Jason Fried and David Heinemeier Hansson (Crown Business)

- *Apprenticeship Patterns: Guidance for the Aspiring Software Craftsman* (*http://bit.ly/apprenticeship_patterns*) by Dave Hoover and Adewale Oshineye (O'Reilly)

- *Quiet: The Power of Introverts in a World That Can't Stop Talking* by Susan Cain (Crown)

- *Fearless Change: Patterns for Introducing New Ideas* by Mary Lynn Manns (Addison-Wesley)

- *The Art & Adventure of Beekeeping* by Ormond Aebi (Rodale Press)

- "Maker's Schedule, Manager's Schedule" (*http://bit.ly/makerssched*) by Paul Graham

- *The Art of Readable Code* (*http://bit.ly/readable_code*) by Dustin Boswell and Trevor Foucher (O'Reilly)

- *Mastery: The Keys to Success and Long-Term Fulfillment* by George Leonard (Plume)

- "The Significance of Task Significance: Job Performance Effects, Relational Mechanisms, and Boundary Conditions" (2008) by Adam M. Grant (Journal of Applied Psychology 93:1, pp. 108–124)

- *Project Retrospectives: A Handbook for Team Reviews* by Norman L. Kerth (Dorset House)

- *The Luck Factor* by Richard Wiseman (Miramax)

- *Search Inside Yourself* by Chade-Meng Tan (HarperOne)

- *Being Geek* (*http://bit.ly/being_geek*) by Michael Lopp (O'Reilly)

- *The Paradox of Choice: Why More Is Less* by Barry Schwartz (Ecco)

- *Critical Chain* by Eliyahu M. Goldratt (North River Press)

- *Delivering Happiness: A Path to Profits, Passion, and Purpose* by Tony Hsieh (Hachette Book Group)

Index

A

abstractions, for hiding complexity, 139
administrative assistants, 116
adult behavior, 102
aggressive cultures, 31
aggressive people, 31
Agile, 36
air cover, for your team, 76
Anna Karenina principle, 102
antipatterns, leadership
    being everyone's friend, 60
    compromising the hiring bar, 60
    hiring pushovers, 57
    ignoring human issues, 59
    ignoring low performers, 58
    treating team like children, 61
Apache Software Foundation (ASF), xxiii,
    127
Apple, 138
Apple TV, 130
application speed, 135
Art of Readable Code, The (Boswell), 45
asynchronous communication, 32
attribution, 46-48
audience, software, 129
authorship, of code, 46-48
average companies, 102-108
    and bad organizations, 106-108
    bad managers in, 103-105
    office politicians in, 105

B

bad companies (see average companies)

bad habits, eliminating, 110
bad managers, 103-105
bad organizations, 106-108, 120-121
barriers to entry
    for first-time users, 131
    latency as, 136
Bell Labs, 3
BigTable, xxiv
Boswell, Dustin, 45
bug trackers, 44
bullet points, in email, 118
bus factor, 6

C

Cain, Susan, 31
calm cultures, 31
calm leadership, 64-66
calmness, when dealing with poisonous
    people, 93
catalyst, leader as, 66-68
celebrity, 4
chain of command, 103
chain of gears, org chart as, 64
chaos, 75
chat, online, 42-44
children, treating team like, 61
Chromecast, 130
Clance, Pauline Rose, 76
code comments, 45
code reviews, 48
collaboration, dangers of avoiding, 5-10
command and control, 106
commits, code reviews for, 48

Have it your way.

Get even more for your money.

Join the O'Reilly Community, and register the O'Reilly books you own. It's free, and you'll get:

- $4.99 ebook upgrade offer
- 40% upgrade offer on O'Reilly print books
- Membership discounts on books and events
- Free lifetime updates to ebooks and videos
- Multiple ebook formats, DRM FREE
- Participation in the O'Reilly community
- Newsletters
- Account management
- 100% Satisfaction Guarantee

Signing up is easy:

1. Go to: oreilly.com/go/register
2. Create an O'Reilly login.
3. Provide your address.
4. Register your books.

Note: English-language books only

To order books online:
oreilly.com/store

For questions about products or an order:
orders@oreilly.com

To sign up to get topic-specific email announcements and/or news about upcoming books, conferences, special offers, and new technologies:
elists@oreilly.com

For technical questions about book content:
booktech@oreilly.com

To submit new book proposals to our editors:
proposals@oreilly.com

O'Reilly books are available in multiple DRM-free ebook formats. For more information:
oreilly.com/ebooks

O'REILLY®

CPSIA information can be obtained at www.ICGtesting.com
Printed in the USA
BVOW06s0849141015

422442BV00022B/132/P